OPTIONS FOR ELECTRONIC MAIL

by Libby Trudell
with
Janet Bruman
and
Dennis Oliver

Knowledge Industry Publications, Inc.

Information and Communications Management Guides

Options for Electronic Mail

Library of Congress Cataloging in Publication Data

Trudell, Libby.
Options for electronic mail.

Bibliography: p.
Includes index.
1. Electronic mail systems. I. Bruman, Janet.
II. Oliver, Dennis. III. Title.
HE6239.E54T78 1984 384.1'4 84-15418
ISBN 0-86729-105-2
ISBN 0-86729-104-4 (pbk.)

Printed in the United States of America

10 9 8 7 6 5 4 3 2 1

Table of Contents

List of Tables and Figures

Preface

What is electronic mail? What can it do to improve communications and productivity in your working environment? What do you need to know in order to choose the best type of system for your particular needs? Organizations of all kinds are increasingly faced with these and other questions raised by the availability of new modes of communications. The purpose of this book is to introduce the reader with limited technical background to the capabilities and characteristics of electronic mail systems (EMS).

Until the 1970s, electronic communications services were provided almost exclusively by regulated carrier services such as Western Union and ITT. By simply acquiring a telex machine, it was possible to send and receive messages directly to and from any other organization with a telex number. Today there are far more options to choose from. The 1980s offer communications services with far greater flexibility, from a bewildering number of service suppliers. Choosing the right type of EMS to meet local needs has the potential to enhance service dramatically. However, there is equal potential for mismatching service capability with actual needs. A mismatch can be expensive, in terms of user frustration as well as actual cost.

WHAT EMS CAN DO FOR YOU

This book is intended to help you avoid a costly mistake by providing a framework for comparing the many different approaches to initiating electronic mail systems that are currently available to business and professional organizations. The major categories of electronic mail service are described in a practical, nontheoretical context to give the reader an understanding of the variety of ways in which EMS can be implemented.

Electronic mail is a feasible and cost-effective alternative to current modes of mail delivery in terms of its potential for improving the communications function. The availability of an ever-increasing number of options for implementing EMS makes it likely that there is an option that matches communications needs in most environments. To provide some context for understanding the current EMS environment, Chapter 1 of this book discusses the development of the EMS industry and its relationship to the overall trend toward office automation.

Starting with an overview of the basic characteristics of the messaging and mail functions, Chapter 2 relates these to EMS capabilities and discusses ways in which EMS can offer new service opportunities. Succeeding chapters examine the major types of electronic mail, describing the basic technology and capabilities of each type of service.

TELECOMMUNICATIONS AND INTERCONNECTION

Regardless of the type of EMS being considered, a telecommunications network of some sort is necessary to the development of a messaging system. To assist the reader in working with the technology, a glossary of telecommunications terms is included in this book. In addition, technical notes providing more detail about specific aspects of telecommunications technology are incorporated into each chapter. It is not the intention of this book to provide extensive technical detail on telecommunications, but rather to suggest some of the telecommunications options which can be utilized in implementing an electronic mail system.

The interconnection of electronic mail systems, providing the capability to transfer messages among various types of mail services and from one telecommunications medium to another, is an issue of major importance to the long-term success of EMS. Because of the numerous developments affecting interconnection capabilities, and the rapid emergence of interface systems which meet this need, interconnection services are described in detail in Chapter 9.

PLANNING FOR THE FUTURE

The field of EMS, like other technology-based services, is a dynamic and rapidly changing one which is currently marked by a large number of new service suppliers. What will happen to all of these new entrants into the market and how can a choice made today be kept current with the changing environment? Some of the developments on the leading edge of the technology are reviewed in the final chapter to provide insight into these questions.

There are some areas relevant to electronic mail that are touched on only briefly in this book. Digital high-speed facsimile, voicemail, digital PBX and other technologies are all becoming available and have the potential for integration with electronic mail services. Because the focus of this work is on providing a practical understanding of basic EMS services, there is no attempt to cover these in detail. However, a brief overview of the outlook for the future provides a sense of where some of these technologies are headed and what types of services are likely to be part of expanded EMS services.

This book is a tool to help the reader understand how electronic mail, and related office automation capabilities, can make working environments more productive and help people deal more effectively with all the information that comes to them. With the basic body of information provided here, the reader will be better equipped to choose the system that is most appropriate to local needs and to successfully integrate electronic communications capabilities into current office procedures.

1

An Overview of Electronic Mail

The typical business manager spends as much as 75% of the day in communications-related activities, according to at least one estimate[1]. The need for more efficient, cost-effective methods of communication is thus obvious and augurs an increasingly important role for electronic mail service (EMS). The entry of MCI into the arena of electronic mail service in late 1983, the growing number of office automation systems which provide communications capabilities, the expense of courier-based delivery systems, the need for more efficient methods of communication—these are only a few of the factors that are changing electronic mail from a novelty to a reality.

The sheer volume of mail delivery is one factor that makes increasing reliance on electronic communication almost inevitable. According to a 1983 report, the U.S. Postal Service delivered more than 113 billion pieces of mail to over 80 million delivery stops in 1982.[2] The information explosion of the 1980s will result in continued expansion of the volume of mail to be handled. This phenomenon—combined with the inability of traditional delivery services to keep up with mail volume, and decreasing costs of new technologies—will be the driving force behind the acceptance of electronic mail as a major communications medium.

SIZE OF THE ELECTRONIC MAIL INDUSTRY

Most industry watchers are predicting that the 1980s will see the widespread acceptance of EMS in the workplace. Various sources reported that there were between 150,000 and 200,000 electronic mailboxes in use by the end of 1982 (including remote access commercial systems as well as in-house systems). At least one analyst projects a more than tenfold increase in the next five years, with an estimated 3 million mailboxes in use by 1987.[3] This estimate, while optimistic, is not unreasonable, in terms of the changing configuration of office equipment.

Computer-based EMS

This rapid increase will result from two converging factors: 1.) The need for faster and more efficient communications services and 2.) the increased availability of personal computers and other communicating devices in the office. The installed base of personal computers was approaching 3 million at the end of 1983 and growing at a rate in excess of 50,000 per month. An estimated 80% were purchased for business applications. In addition, most word processing and office automation systems are now being delivered with communications capability. If this trend continues, by the end of the 1980s, almost every office worker, from support staff to management, will have easy access to a terminal that can be used for EMS.

Although it is difficult to estimate the number of microcomputer-based EMS systems currently in operation, the number of microcomputers equipped with modems is shown as a leading indicator of the potential for this type of EMS service.

Telex and Other Systems

In addition to the computer-based EMS services, the large installed base of telex terminals represents an important segment of the electronic mail market. Another element of electronic communication is found in the use of facsimile equipment, which provides a method for transmitting the graphic image of a page. Figure 1.1 illustrates the current size of the electronic mail market in its various forms compared to total U.S. Postal Service mail delivery and the expected growth in the 1980s.

A 1983 report showed that the world-wide market for electronic mail services is expected to reach $5 billion by 1985.[4] The opportunity to gain a foothold in this potentially lucrative service market has inspired the offering of many new electronic mail services, ranging from the U.S. Post Office E-COM service to a variety of microcomputer-based systems. Additional systems and service options are certain to be introduced by some of the giants of the computer and telecommunications industry, as companies such as IBM prepare for entry into the communications market, and AT&T introduces its line of personal computers.

Choosing among these services, developing a strategy for integrating electronic communications capability into the office routine and linking them with a plethora of external services will be a significant task for the business manager in the 1980s. Making the best use of these new capabilities as they are provided will be a challenge for every office worker.

Figure 1.1: The Electronic Mail Market

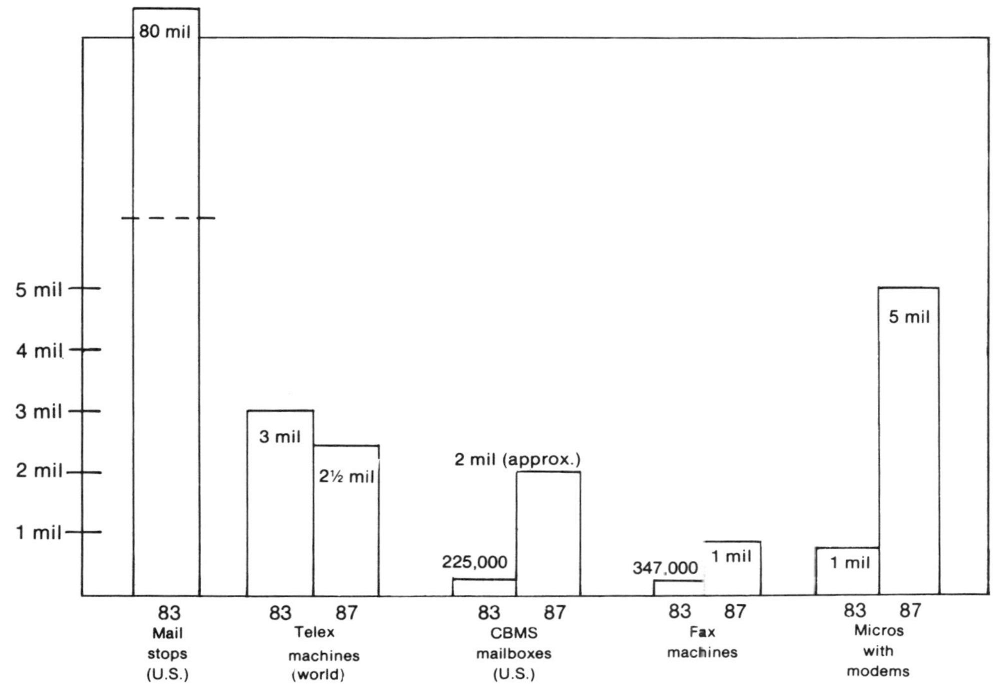

*Note: No 1987 estimate for total U.S. mail delivery stops available.
Sources: ITT, U.S. Postal Service estimates, 1983.

ELECTRONIC MAIL AND OFFICE AUTOMATION

In addressing the functions and capabilities of electronic mail, it is important to keep in mind that for most business environments, implementation of an electronic mail system is really only a part of the larger question of office automation. An examination of the possibilities for improving office communications electronically should include an examination of all office functions. Certainly, office automation is a big business. According to a 1983 report, office automation equipment users spent nearly eight billion dollars in 1982, and this is expected to double by 1987.[5]

It is outside the scope of this book to cover integrated office automation in detail. However, a quick review will help to place electronic mail in an appropriate perspective.

The Office of the Future

The term "office of the future" was coined in the 1970s to describe a whole complex of office automation capabilities. Its hallmark was to be the presence of a computer terminal on the desk of nearly every white-collar worker, from secretary to top management. According to many predictions, the office of the future would be the most exciting and most beneficial development to occur in the business environment. With the office of the future, computer applications would move beyond payroll, billing, inventory and accounting to encompass capabilities such as word processing, access to personal databases, electronic mail and computer conferencing.

All of these functions were seen as integral parts of the new automated environment. However, the potential for increased efficiency was envisioned most strongly in the area of communications services for management as opposed to word processing services for support staff. This is pointed out clearly by statistics published in 1979 showing that the secretary/typist functions supported by word processing account for only 6% of labor costs of U.S. business, while nonclerical labor costs amount to 66% of total costs.[6] Technology in the form of computerized mail is particularly well-suited to the automation of these nonclerical functions. The potential for cost savings in use of electronic mail is particularly high because, as noted previously, managers spend such a high percentage of their time in communications-related activities.

The Present Situation

Despite the glowing predictions about what the office of the future would do to increase white-collar productivity, office automation in 1983 was still largely synonymous with word processing, and word processing still the application that usually motivated the introduction of computer-based equipment in the office environment. Investment in office automation thus far has concentrated on machines performing this single function. In many offices, those administrators or executives who could benefit most from electronic mail have remained largely unaware of it.

The Impact of Microprocessing

However, there are indications that the time is rapidly approaching when electronic mail and related automated functions will more fully penetrate the business environment. This is largely due to the innovations in microprocessing which will enable an individual workstation to perform a range of office automation functions. This workstation will, in some cases, be a telephone terminal, which can be used both for voice communications and access to computer systems, and in some cases be a microcomputer or other device. Although only 20% of all white-collar workers now have an electronic keyboard device, 80% are expected to have one by 1986.[7]

These executive/professional workstations will help managers take information in any form, manipulate it and format it in the best medium for presentation. In addition to electronic mail, the executive workstation will probably perform word processing, personal computing, administrative support functions such as creating calendars and directories, database management and connection to external systems. Such multi-functional equipment will revolutionize offices in the next few years, and the use of electronic mail will be an important part of this revolution.

Clearly, electronic mail is only one aspect of the management support functions which computerized systems can provide. However, the introduction of an electronic mail system, with its potential to affect white-collar productivity, can in fact be the most significant element of any office automation plan.

THE ROLE OF COMMUNICATIONS NETWORKS

An important aspect of any discussion of electronic mail is the role of telecommunications. Phenomenal changes in telecommunications technologies and capabilities have occurred in the last decade. At the same time, the computer industry has reached maturity, and a synergy between the two technologies has produced powerful new applications. The convergence of communications and computer technology continues to bring about new combinations and capabilities for transferring data from one place to another.

Two Basic Telecommunications Networks

Today's confusing mix of electronic mail services has developed from two basic telecommunications network options: the telex and the telephone.

Telex Network

Telex was the first successful technology for long distance data communications. Developed for the purpose of transmitting text messages, the telex became the standard for non-voice communication, with the provision of telex service regulated in the United States by the Federal Communications Commission (FCC) to licensed carriers. The services of the International Record Carriers (IRCs), which are described in more detail in Chapter 3, are still an important element in the electronic mail mix.

Telephone Network

The telephone network, which by the middle of the 20th century reached into essentially every home and business in the United States, has far surpassed the telex networks in number of users. Operating through analog transmission of voice signals and designed specifically for audio communications, the telephone network in many ways is a clumsy instrument for data transmission. (See Technical Note 1:1.) Yet, because of its universal availability and relative flexibility, the telephone network is now the major supplier of computer telecommunications service, as well as voice communications. Standard telephone service, or Direct Distance Dialing (DDD), provides the basic telecommunications framework for most of the EMS services available.

> Technical Note 1:1
>
> Analog transmission makes use of audio frequencies to represent the sounds of the voice. These frequencies follow a pattern which is analogous to the actual voice signal, and which can be interpreted by the telephone instrument at the receiving end, and converted into the actual sound of the voice. Data that are formatted for computer processing, however, are stored in digital form (that is, encoded as ones and zeros) and then must be converted to an audio frequency in order to be transmitted over voice lines through telephone installations.

THE EVOLUTION OF EMS

The existence of these two parallel systems, both handling large volumes of message traffic and data communication, has contributed to the development of various specialized electronic mail services. Message handling equipment and services evolved to enhance and supplement the basic data transmission capability available from each network. There are devices which receive and store incoming telex messages until an operator is available to print them out, "intelligent" computer terminals* which are capable of transmitting

*A "dumb" computer terminal is one that can only enter or retrieve data, as opposed to an "intelligent" terminal which can also do calculations and rearrange, or process, information.

messages from one terminal to another over phone lines, computer systems which control and enhance data communications and many others.

Having been developed to serve particular applications, these devices and systems in their original versions were usually capable of linking with only one type of network. One of the most significant current trends in EMS services is the tendency toward devices and systems that support both telephone and telex technology, or that provide an interface between the two. Not only have these developments added many new products and choices to the EMS scene, but they are beginning to blur the line between the two networks. As schematically indicated in Figure 1.2, the evolutionary path of EMS is toward services that can transmit messages over both networks.

Figure 1.2: The Evolution of EMS Services

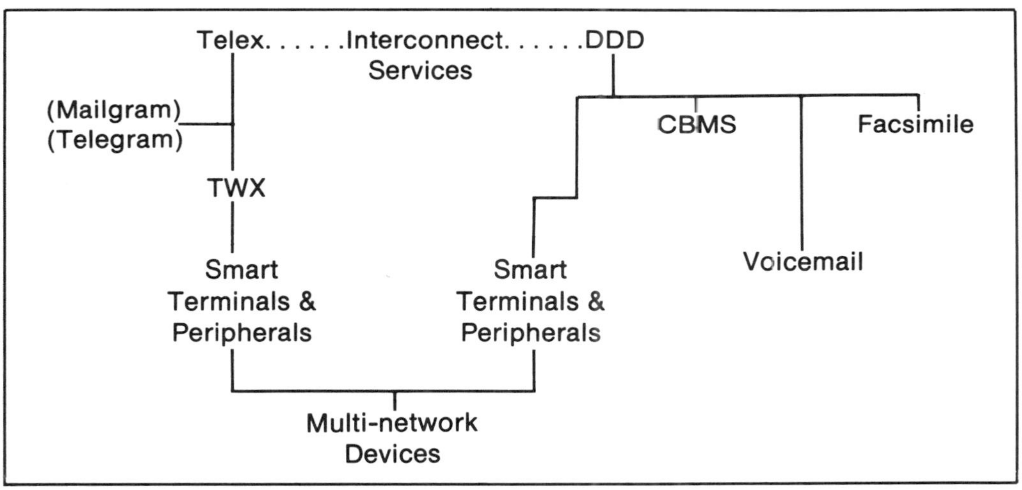

Electronic mail services have developed in stages from:

1. *Simple* communications networks with little intelligence or capability for message control;

2. Services with *centralized intelligence* controlling the entire network for increased message-handling capabilities;

3. Services based on *distributed intelligence,* with message-handling capabilities and storage capabilities at the local workstation.

CURRENT OPTIONS FOR EMS

Today, we are at a point in the development of mail services in which increasingly sophisticated, intelligent hardware coupled with continued advances in network interface capabilities provides numerous options for EMS.

The major categories of electronic mail service will be described in detail in Chapters 3 through 9. They are presented in an evolutionary order, starting with the telex networks.

- Telex and TWX. Traditional telex message services, such as Western Union and ITT, are developing new services to meet the more sophisticated communications market.
- Computer-based message systems (CBMS). Commercial or in-house systems offering services by which text of messages is transmitted to a central computer and stored for pick-up by the recipient.
- Local electronic mail networks, in which computing and communications operations are handled at each local workstation.
- Message processing workstations and intelligent peripherals. Microprocessor-based communications equipment which can be used to send and receive messages directly from one site to another, over either teletype, telephone or other networks.
- Software systems. Off-the-shelf software which can be used to turn general purpose equipment into a communications device.
- Interconnection services. External services to link diverse electronic mail systems.

SUMMARY

Electronic mail is a growing industry and has the potential to improve communications capabilities in many work environments. However, EMS should not be implemented without consideration of the overall approach to automated office support systems for the organization. There are many different types of EMS systems, but all developed from the basic telecommunications services provided by the telex and telephone networks. The interconnection between these two types of services is a major force behind the evolution of EMS.

Regardless of the type of EMS chosen, certain fundamental message-handling functions must be provided by the system. To lay a basic framework for comparing the characteristics of specific types of systems, Chapter 2 reviews the functions of a mail system and describes the ways in which electronic mail differs from traditional delivery methods.

FOOTNOTES

1. Stuart L. Mathison, "Telecommunications: Linking up for Greater Productivity," *Administrative Management* 42 (3) (March 1981): 33-34, 74.

2. William Bolger, "USPS and Mailers Can Be Partners in Progress," *ZIP* 6 (1) (January 1983): 25, 35-36.

3. *Electronic Mail* (Framingham, MA: International Data Corp., 1983).

4. Lloyd Reaume, "Terminals, Telephones and Technology," *Computer Data* 8 (4) (April 1983): 4-5.

5. K.Hafner, "Study Examines Future of OA Market," *Computerworld* 17 (36) (September 5, 1983): 73.

6. Ronald A. Frank, "Computerized Mail Seen Future Benefit," *Computerworld* 12 (41) (October 1978): 18, 23.

7. Ronald Mercer, "Office Automation: Managers Will Have to Change," *Computing Canada* 9 (8) (April 1983): 15, 24-25.

2

Electronic versus Traditional Mail Service

Any organization considering implementing an EMS service must first examine just what an electronic mail system is and how it differs from traditional mail delivery systems. Next, it is important to identify what the basic objectives of mail delivery in general are, and how electronic and traditional mail services measure up in these areas. This chapter will examine each of these areas, and will also present some guidelines for evaluating the cost of EMS versus traditional mail. It serves as a framework for understanding the differences among the various EMS options discussed in the balance of this book.

HOW EMS WORKS

In order to learn more about the basic technology of electronic mail, we will examine how an EMS compares to a manual delivery system—in terms of how messages are created, how they are delivered and how they are handled after being received.

Creating the Message

The primary difference between traditional mail and EMS is the medium of communication. Instead of delivering a piece of paper with information written on it, an electronic mail system delivers just the information itself. In order to accomplish this, the information must be translated into a format that can be transmitted through a communications network. Instead of typing text onto a piece of paper, the sender keys the text into a device which translates it into an electronic format. Typically, this device is a computer terminal, with a keyboard much like a typewriter keyboard, and the capability to display text either on a screen (known as a cathode ray tube or CRT) or on a printer.

Even in offices where an EMS has never previously been considered for the delivery of text to a remote location, terminals connected to specialized computers designed for word processing and other applications are often standard equipment. These systems are proliferating because they provide tremendous advantages for ease of editing, revision and repeated use of standardized formats in the creation of all sorts of documents in-house. In many business environments, a significant percentage of all correspondence is already created on word processors in an electronic form which can be transmitted through a communications network. (See Technical Note 2:1.)

Technical Note 2:1

The electronic form being discussed here can be thought of as a code into which all the alphabetic and other types of characters are converted so that a computer can interpret them. Computers can only understand numbers, so each character is translated into a number. In fact, computers can only understand the numbers "0"and "1," so each character is expressed as a seven-digit combination of zeros and ones. For example, the letter "T" is translated into 1010100. Each digit in this code is called a "bit" and the entire numeric combination which expresses one character is called a "byte." This code is the American Standard for Communications Information Interchange (ASCII).

Textual Material

Most of the information which passes through the mail is textual and is easily translated into an electronic format by being keyed. The ASCII code provides the capability to represent 128 different characters. These include all standard alphabetic and numeric characters, plus punctuation and various special control characters or codes (for example, a code that tells the computer that it is time to move down to the next line—the equivalent of a carriage return on a typewriter). These control codes also handle various formatting requirements for the printed text, such as form feed and end-of-text.

Visual Images

For some applications, there is also the requirement to transmit pictures, graphics and other visual images. Information of this type is far more difficult to translate into a format that can be transmitted electronically. Ordinary word processors and other text editing systems usually do not provide a way to translate graphic images. Special facsimile equipment, which can break down an actual image into a set of signals representing the dark, light and shaded areas, is needed. These signals can then be transmitted and reassembled back into a visual image when received.

In order to achieve an adequate reproduction of the original visual image, it is necessary to scan the image and break it down into thousands of segments. Instead of the seven-digit number which serves to identify a character of text to the computer, it takes many more signals to represent an equivalent amount of information through facsimile reproduction. Facsimile transmission and receipt requires specialized equipment, and may take longer to transmit than keyed text because more bits of information are being sent. At this time, only a few specialized systems offer integration of facsimile and other graphics transmission systems with standard text transmission.

Transmitting the Message

Once the message has been translated into an electronic code, it can be transmitted in that format over communications lines. A communications line can be just an ordinary telephone line, the most widespread and easily available type of network. However, there are also several types of communications networks designed specifically for electronic data communications. The most commonly available ones are Tymnet, Telenet and Uninet, all of which employ a technology called "packet switching" to insure high-speed, error-free data transmission. It is possible to connect to these networks by making a local phone call in most parts of the United States (and, increasingly, throughout the world). These networks support all kinds of communications, whether between an individual and a computer or from computer to computer.

Despite the fact that packet switched networks can accommodate very high-speed communications, transmission speeds available for personal communication through EMS systems are generally limited to a range of 10 to 120 characters per second (cps) or 1200 baud. (See Technical Note 2.2.) This is because of the limitations imposed by 1.) accessing the data communication network through voice grade telephone lines and 2.) the technology of the equipment currently available for use with standard phone lines.

Although voice grade phone lines continue to support most data communications, many new technologies for data communications are now coming into use, including microwave, satellite, fiber optics and coaxial cable. These high-speed and high-capacity technologies are being integrated into the networks maintained by both AT&T and the various data communication utilities.

> Technical Note 2:2
>
> The term "1200 baud" or 120 cps refers to the number of electronic pulses or bits which can be transmitted per second. Text being transmitted in standard ASCII format usually requires 10 bits per character to accommodate the seven bit code which represents that character, plus three additional pulses. The extras are a "start bit," which is a signal to the computer that a new character is coming; a "stop bit," which signals the end of the character; and a "parity bit," which is used by the computer to check and make sure that all the bits were correctly received. When transmitting 10-bit ASCII-coded text, 1200 baud is equivalent to 120 characters of text per second. The most common transmission speeds over standard phone lines are 30 and 120 cps but 240 is now beginning to be supported by the public data network.

In some cases, it may be possible to develop private networks or to tie into one that is being developed locally. The use of data communications technology that supports higher transmission speeds will be increasingly important as an organization's volume of electronic message traffic increases.

Delivering the Mail

The methods by which mail is delivered in an EMS system may be divided into two general categories: direct delivery and centralized delivery.

Direct Delivery

Information may be delivered directly from the sender to the recipient, or from one point in the communications network to another. The teletype services available from Western Union and International Telephone and Telegraph (ITT) are an example of direct connect mail networks. Such direct connect systems offer the advantage of immediate delivery of mail, since messages are sent and received simultaneously. However, these services also tend to require specialized, dedicated equipment. Figure 2.1 provides a schematic representation of the operation of a direct or point-to-point network.

Centralized Delivery

The other general category of mail delivery is a centralized or "pick-up" delivery system in which all messages are sent to a central storage area rather than directly to the recipient. A host computer generally performs this

Figure 2.1: Direct Delivery Network

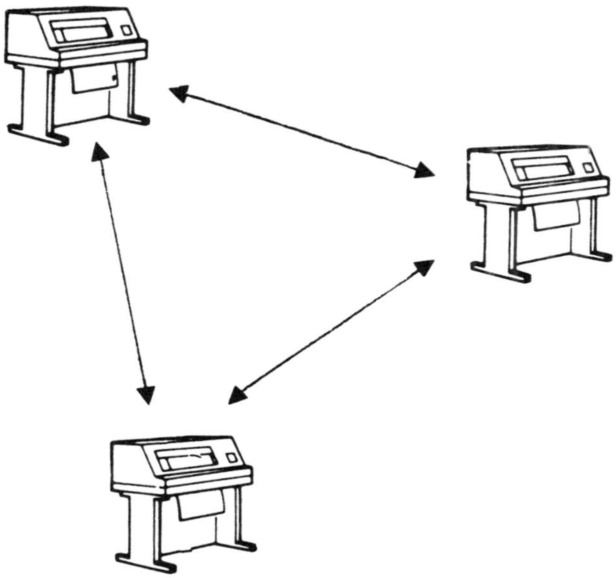

storage function, acting like an electronic post office to hold the messages until the recipient is ready to pick them up. In some cases, the computer can be instructed to forward the messages to the recipient automatically or at a specified future time. In either case, the sender is relieved of the necessity to make a direct, real-time connection with the recipient.

When comparing a direct delivery system to a centralized one, it may be helpful to use the analogy of a postal delivery service which delivers the mail to your door versus having a post office box to which you go to get your mail. If the mail in your post office box is never picked up, it remains undelivered. Fortunately, it is easier to check your electronic mailbox than to make a trip to the post office! Figure 2.2 provides a schematic illustration of a centralized delivery network.

Reading and Handling the Mail

In order for the recipient to actually read the transmitted message or information, it must be displayed in some format. The receiving point may be a printing terminal, a microcomputer, a word processor or some other device. One of the significant differences between standard mail and EMS is that the format of the received EMS message depends very much upon the type of equipment used to receive the message.

Figure 2.2: Centralized Delivery Network

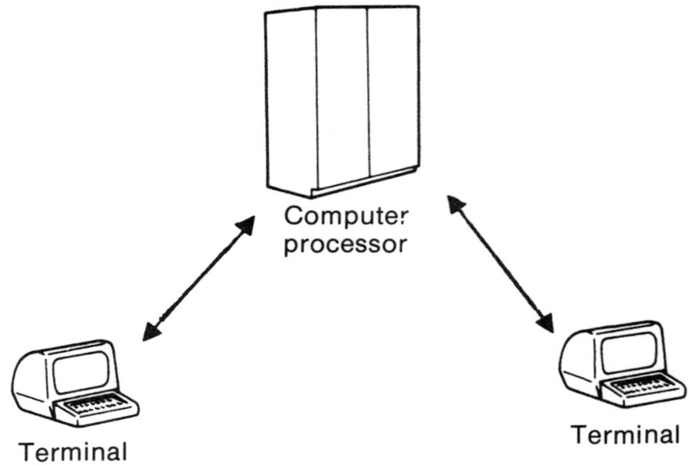

If the message is printed out onto paper, it is once again a separate physical item which can be stored in a file cabinet, interfiled with mail received through other channels. However, it is also possible to maintain a copy of the message in the electronic format, either in a local storage device, or through the services offered by the mail system used. If storage costs are reasonable, and if a method for accessing the messages as needed is available, an online, electronic filing system may begin to replace, or at least supplement, paper files. (See Technical Note 2:3.)

Technical Note 2:3

The term "online" refers to information to which you can have immediate access through a terminal or other interactive device. Technological developments of the past 15 years have led to the development of systems that support the storage and retrieval of massive amounts of information, which may be accessed online by many people at one time. Information can also be stored in an electronic or machine-readable form which is not immediately accessible; such computer environments are referred to as offline or batch processing systems.

The advantages of maintaining online files are numerous. For example, if you have received a message that you know will be of interest to others, you can transmit a copy of the message without having to rekey the text. You can also add a note of your own to the original message, or perhaps add different comments for the different people to whom the message is being forwarded. You can also reply to the sender and include a copy of the original message to provide a context for your remarks. Basically, online storage allows repeated revision, manipulation and reuse of the same information over and over again as it is needed in different situations.

COMPARING EMS AND TRADITIONAL MAIL

The primary purpose of any mail system, electronic or otherwise, is the delivery of information from one person to another, as quickly as possible. A mail system must also be dependable, with procedures that ensure delivery of an item to the correct recipient, and offer some measure of security. Because the information to be delivered may be in any format—from personal correspondence and business memos, to purchase orders and invoices, to full-length reports and documents—a mail system must be flexible. Finally, the system must be universal; that is, it must support the delivery of mail to any destination.

For the majority of us, the most familiar way to accomplish these aims is to write or type the information on a piece of paper and send that piece of paper through the postal system. In this delivery mode, the same piece of paper is handled through various switch points and is physically delivered to the addressee.

Speed of Delivery

Because of the delays inherent in travel time and handling, it is rare for mail to be delivered through a postal system in less than two days, and regular delivery across country may take four to six days. Special overnight delivery services are available, but their labor-intensive nature makes such services very expensive. In comparison, one of the most important characteristics of electronic mail is the capability to transfer information instantly. Because electronic delivery is immediate, deadlines can be met more easily, questions can be answered without delay and work can be completed faster and more efficiently.

Reliability of Delivery

Speed is an important consideration, but perhaps even more important is the assurance that a piece of correspondence has actually been delivered. Traditional mail systems provide no receipt capability, except in the special case of certified mail. To determine when an important letter or order has arrived at its destination, it is necessary to just wait for a reply or, if it is really important, to contact the recipient. Many electronic mail systems, however, provide a reporting mechanism that allows verification of the precise time that the mail was read by the recipient as a standard feature. This is of crucial importance in a business environment where verification of the receipt of a report or bid can be the difference between making or losing a sale.

Security

Another basic requirement for mail systems is protection from having private data exposed to the wrong eyes. While traditional mail systems provide adequate privacy protection for most applications, mail delivery through an EMS can be designed for additional security features, so that only authorized personnel can gain access to certain types of information. This kind of protection can be particularly valuable at higher management levels.

Flexibility and Universal Delivery

Electronic mail can offer improvements in delivery speed, reliability and security compared to standard mail delivery. There are still two other basic features of a mail system identified at the beginning of this section: the capability for universal delivery, and the capability to deliver materials in all kinds of formats.

In these two areas, EMS services can present problems. At present, there is no universal electronic mail system that can cover the wide delivery range of the regular postal service. However, there is more and more evidence that the process of standardizing electronic mail formats, which has recently begun, will continue and eventually offer widespread possibilities for interconnection of mail systems. (Chapter 9 will discuss this topic in detail.)

The capability to deliver mail in formats of all kinds is another area where EMS has limitations compared to traditional mail. As discussed earlier in this chapter, special technologies are required to transmit graphics information and other specialized formats, and these usually require special equipment or transmission facilities.

NEW SERVICES PROVIDED BY EMS

When comparing EMS to traditional mail service, it is also important to keep in mind the improvements to existing service that EMS can provide. In some business environments, an EMS service represents the potential for improved services by providing capabilities that simply are not possible with traditional mail. To illustrate this point, let's look at some typical patterns of mail activity and see how these could be improved.

Improved Internal Communications

In most business environments, there are two basic categories of messages: internal communications between departments or divisions of the same company or organization; and external communications with other organizations, customers, suppliers, etc. Traditionally, the first type of communication is handled through personal delivery systems within the same building, combined with courier or postal service for intraorganizational mail to other locations. This mixture may result in discrepancies between the time in which information is received on-site and when it is received in field offices and other off-site locations.

With electronic mail, information is delivered to everyone on the distribution list at the same time, regardless of the location of recipients. Thus, each salesperson can be updated on new prices as soon as these are decided, each department can receive inventory listings and each field office can be kept in touch with the central office and with each other, regardless of distance or location. This capability is particularly important for staff members who travel frequently and who may be difficult to reach by either phone or regular mail.

Another feature of internal mail is the need to route materials among a group of people to gather comments and generate a response. When one physical piece of mail is being routed, this process is slow, and annotating the same document can become messy. In an electronic mail system, it may be possible to store the document that is being reviewed in the system so that everyone can review it and add comments. In this way, one slow person on the routing list does not hold up the review; everyone gets a chance to look at it at the same time, and a more thorough review process can take place in a shorter time frame.

Improved External Communications

External mail presents a different set of considerations, since it requires the essentially universal delivery capability of a standard postal system. It is far more difficult to develop a coherent approach to the implementation of EMS among diverse organizations than to develop it within an organization. However, the development of electronic communications capabilities with major suppliers or large customers can enhance relationships with these key external contacts by facilitating delivery of orders and creating a direct connection for the quick resolution of problems.

In certain business and professional environments, participation in EMS networks with associates, such as fellow members of the local Chamber of Commerce or a national professional organization, can improve the flow of useful information and provide new opportunities for interaction. There are relatively few examples of the use of electronic communications in this type of environment as yet, but the proliferation of in-house systems will certainly fuel experiments of this kind.

COMPARING COSTS

Cost is an important factor in the increasing popularity of EMS communications services. A study by the Dartnell Institute of Business Research placed the cost of a first class business letter in 1982 at $7.11, which represented an increase of 100% since 1974. This estimate included the cost of dictation time by an executive, secretarial time to type and file, overhead and fixed costs, materials, and postage and mail handling costs.

Of course, a number of these cost elements are present in any type of mail service, whether electronic communications methods are used or not. For example, overhead and fixed costs are likely to remain the same. Also, even if an executive keys in a message directly instead of dictating it, his or her time is still a cost factor.

However, electronic options provide the opportunity to create a different mix of cost elements by reducing secretarial support requirements or handling costs. With many short or informal communications, EMS is both less expensive in terms of total personnel cost, and more efficient.

EMS vs. Traditional Mail

Because the electronic mail equipment and services used vary from organization to organization, it is very difficult, if not impossible, to place a meaningful dollar figure on the cost of an electronic message as compared to, for example, a first class letter. However, it is possible to estimate the transmission, or delivery, costs of electronic and traditional mail.

Table 2.1 provides estimated transmission costs for several types of communications services. Estimates are provided for messages of 500 characters (equivalent to a short note of 100 words) and for a longer message of 2500 characters, equivalent to an average business letter. None of these figures include the cost of labor, overhead, materials or equipment, all of which would have to be factored into a full estimate for a working environment. All of these estimates reflect domestic U.S. charges; international delivery would be more expensive in most cases. Additional details about the cost and service capability for all electronic communications services will be provided in later chapters. A brief description of each type is provided in the table to assist in evaluating the figures given.

EMS vs. Voice Communications

It is also useful to compare EMS costs with the cost of voice communications, since EMS provides a similar capability for immediate contact. In addition to the standard service charges, phone service bears the hidden cost of telephone tag and message taking. A fairly low percentage of all business calls are completed on the first attempt (some studies place it as low as 28%), resulting in a high cost both for repeated call placement and for lost productive time. Therefore, when reviewing telephone and EMS costs, whether local or long distance, it is appropriate to multiply telephone charges by a factor of two or three for a realistic comparison.

Improved service capability, rather than cost reduction, is generally the main reason for implementing electronic communication service. However, as discussed below, for many businesses, EMS can be a factor in overall cost reduction due to efficiency and, in some cases, actual communications costs.

EVALUATING EMS

For most organizations today, the first decision to be made regarding EMS is not which option to choose, but whether to implement an electronic mail system. As mentioned earlier, this decision is rarely based on cost factors alone—one exception might be an organization that has an extraordinarily high volume of message traffic. Any organization considering electronic mail must carefully examine applications, in addition to costs. This requires

Table 2.1: Mail Delivery Cost Comparisons

Type of Mail	500 Characters	2500 Characters
1. First Class Mail	$ .20	$ .20
2. Express Mail	9.85	9.85
3. Western Union Mailgram	7.45	17.45
4. TWX: 1983	1.40	4.20
1984*	2.80	5.60
5. Telex: 1983	1.22	3.30
1984*	2.62	4.70
6. EMS- OnTyme	.26	1.33
DIALCOM	.82	4.12

*Estimates

1. Regular postal service.

2. Express mail overnight delivery. Any overnight delivery or courier service could also be compared in this category.

3. Western Union Mailgram. Priority mail sent electronically through the Western Union network to a major post office in the vicinity of the recipient, and actually delivered by first class mail. Rate shown is for the standard over-the-counter service or for mailgrams telephoned in to an operator. Differing prices apply to mailgrams generated at terminals and through other systems (see Chapter 9).

4. TWX. A message from one TWX terminal to another over dedicated Western Union lines. The figures given are for flat rates plus monthly line rental charges, which average from $.70 to $1.25 a month for both TWX and telex. The monthly line rental cost is expected to rise sharply in 1984, as shown in the 1984 estimate.

5. Telex. A message from one telex terminal to another. The figures given are for flat rates plus monthly line rental charges. An increase in monthly line rental costs for telex in 1984 is also expected (see Chapter 3).

6. EMS. Estimates are shown for two popular commercial EMS systems (see Chapter 4).

a thorough analysis of how an organization uses the mail. The key questions to ask are:

- How much mail does the organization send?

- What delivery means does it use (and why)?
- What material does it send?

The volume of mail, its physical characteristics (i.e., text, graphics, etc.), whether it is primarily inter- or intraorganizational and how the mail is sent (first class, primarily through courier services, etc.)—all will have a bearing on whether the organization chooses to implement an EMS and, if so, which options it will choose.[1]

SUMMARY

This chapter has reviewed the basic functions of mail as a mode of information transfer, and has examined the ways in which electronic mail fulfills the function of message creation, delivery and handling. There are two basic types of mail delivery systems: point-to-point and centralized retrieval. With this background, we are now ready to examine specific types of electronic mail delivery in more detail.

FOOTNOTES

1. Stephen Connell and Jan A. Galbraith, *Electronic Mail: A Revolution in Business Communications* (White Plains, NY: Knowledge Industry Publications, Inc., 1982), pp. 19-23.

3

Telex and TWX Networks

With more than 3 million telex machines installed and working worldwide, the international telex network is without question the most widespread and generally available electronic mail network currently in operation. As of early 1984, telex service was available from 156 countries around the world. International communications capability is a primary characteristic of telex service, and the reason why it is still an important element of electronic communication despite the fact that far more flexible and powerful communications systems exist.

This chapter will describe how telex services work, the organizations that provide them and the regulatory/policy-making agencies that seek to control them. First, we offer a brief historical note on the development of telex.

THE TELEGRAPH: THE FIRST INCARNATION OF ELECTRONIC MAIL

Telex is an outgrowth of the telegraph. Thus, the birth of electronic mail is often set at May 24, 1844, when Samuel Morse demonstrated his first crude telegraph device and sent the first public telegram consisting of the text "What hath God wrought?" (The quotation was selected for the occasion by Annie Ellsworth, daughter of the U.S. Patent Commissioner.)

Morse conceived of the telegraph in 1832; however, it took him 12 years to perfect the idea into a working model and to convince the U.S. Congress to expend $30,000 for an experimental telegraph circuit between Washington and Baltimore. Morse tried to sell the invention to the U.S. government for $100,000 but officials considered it an impractical toy and it was left to private enterprise to develop.

The first telegraph circuit used underground wires, a mechanical transmitting device and a moving strip of paper tape to record the dots and dashes of Morse's code. In 1846 Morse and his backers extended the circuit to New York City and eventually sold licenses to other companies to provide telegraph service among different locations. Soon all major cities were connected by telegraph and a new industry had been born.

By 1856 telegraph operators had learned the Morse code well enough to bypass the mechanical recording devices and were transmitting and receiving messages by ear using a telegraph key and sounder. The return to mechanical recording devices and underground lines would take several more decades, an ironic footnote to the electronic communications story.

Within 50 years the telegraph and the railroad had conquered the North American continent, and the worldwide use of telegraph lines for the communication of vital information had become common. The telegraph was the first electronic (electric, really) mail service and it changed the way the world did business. The fragile copper telegraph wire was the first step toward the global village. Together with the railroad, the telegraph was a crucial instrument of the industrial revolution.

TELEX: THE SECOND INCARNATION

The telegraph soon spawned other long-distance communication technologies including transatlantic cable, radio (wireless) and teleprinter devices. By the turn of the century, the public telegraph network was so busy that Western Union was forced to develop the automatic mechanical teleprinter device and a network of lines to connect them. The machines and network together are the basic components of the network and service internationally known as the TELegraph EXchange or telex. The telex network and service essentially replaced the telegraph system being used for national and international communications.

CHARACTERISTICS OF TELEX

Equipment

Telex machines consist of a keyboard, a printing mechanism that will print incoming messages (and keyboard input) on roll or fanfold paper, and a translation device that interprets either keyboard strokes or incoming electrical signals as baudot codes (see Technical Note 3:1). Telex machines usually have an attached paper-tape reader and punch that enables an operator to store received messages or prepare messages that are going to be sent, prior to making a connection with the recipient machine.

Transmission

Telex machines can be connected to a telex circuit in two different ways. They may be permanently connected to a single line or circuit, (dedicated or

> Technical Note 3:1
>
> Telex technology uses a five-level coding system called baudot, analog electrical signals and dedicated lines (physical circuits). The telex machines that are connected to this dedicated network are mechanical devices that are capable of sending and receiving electrical impulses using the baudot coding scheme and electrical characteristics of the telex circuit.

leased line), or they may be connected to a public telex network and use a telephone-like dialing mechanism to establish a temporary circuit with another machine. In the first case the telex machine can only communicate with other machines on that particular line or circuit. In the second case a telex machine can be used to communicate with any other telex machine on public networks (see Technical Note 3:2).

> Technical Note 3:2
>
> An important operational characteristic of the telex machine is the answerback. The answerback is a string of letters or numbers that is used to identify a particular telex machine or circuit. When a certain electrical signal is sent to a telex machine, that machine responds by sending its answerback. In this way, a caller can verify that he has indeed reached the correct number (telex machine) in the public network. Two telex machines exchanging answerbacks is the basic technique used to prevent the occurrence of wrong numbers.

Limitations of Telex

The telex machine and public network were a success because companies could operate their own communications at a lower cost per message than by using the public telegram delivery service. But there are inherent limitations in the baudot coding scheme and the speed of the telex network. Users are limited to a basic character set of only 64 characters, enough for the upper-case alphabet, a few special characters and punctuation, plus the control characters used by the telex network and other telex machines. There is also a limitation in the speed of transmission. The telex network operates at a speed of 50 baud and is capable of sending or receiving about 10 characters per second. This is the equivalent of 50 or 60 words a minute.

INTERNATIONAL COMMUNICATIONS

Telex remains the international standard for the transmission and communication of messages. In most countries, electronic communication with other nations is managed as a government monopoly.

PTTs

In virtually every country of the world except the United States, telex services are regulated under the basic jurisdiction of the same government agency that regulates postal services and telephones. Generically called Post, Telegraph and Telephone agencies (PTTs), these organizations are responsible for the control and regulation of communications within the country, and for cooperation with other countries in the orderly and consistent handling of international messages. The PTTs also own and operate communications facilities within the nation or subcontract with other companies for equipment and service.

There is some evidence that communications policies abroad are changing. For example, in the U.K. authority is still primarily vested with British Telecom (formerly the telecommunications division of the post office but now an independent corporation), but there has been an attempt to encourage private enterprise. In 1981 a deregulation bill was passed ending the British Telecom monopoly over equipment and transmission services.

FCC

In the United States, private enterprise and public regulation maintain a tenuous balance in the face of rapidly changing technology. In the United States, the Federal Communications Commission (FCC) is the regulatory agency responsible for communications policy and the coordination of communications carriers. The FCC therefore acts in the role of PTT with respect to the various international committees and tariff negotiations.

The FCC is also empowered to license companies to provide and sell international communications services. These companies are called International Record Carriers (IRCs) and are an important component of the electronic mail picture. The pricing and service standards adopted by IRCs and regulated by the FCC and its foreign equivalents, the PTTs, play a critical role in the structure of electronic communications services.

Because of these limitations, the U.S. communications market required a faster and more flexible communications alternative, which arrived in the form of the teletype or TWX network.

TWX: A DOMESTIC NETWORK

After World War II, AT&T introduced its teletypewriter exchange (TWX) service in the United States. This system used a different coding scheme: a seven-level code called ASCII, (American Standard Code for Information Interchange, described in Chapter 2). The advantage over telex was obvious and immediate. The user now had access to 128 characters which constituted "standard" ASCII. There were also another 128 characters that were available in the code, although undefined in the system or the teletype machines supplied to be used with the system (see Technical Note 3:3). This meant the ability to provide both upper and lower-case characters, more special characters and punctuation, and a generally more professional and flexible message capability. Another significant advantage of the TWX service was that it was slightly more than twice as fast as the telex network, operating at 110 baud.

> Technical Note 3:3
>
> As computers were developed into serious business tools during the late 1950s, it became necessary to program them with devices other than the hardwiring techniques then being used by the punched card tabulating industry. The teletypewriter (TTY) subset of the ASCII code (the standard 128-character set used by teletype machines) became the default standard used by many terminal manufacturers. Computer and terminal builders soon began to utilize the "extra"128 characters available in the ASCII code to provide special functions and software capabilities. ASCII, therefore, has both standard and non-standard implementations, and a terminal may use ASCII code but still not be compatible with other ASCII systems.

When Western Union bought the TWX network from AT&T in 1969, there were nearly 40,000 machines on the network, as compared to 26,000 telex machines on Western Union's domestic telex network. Western Union provided protocol and speed conversion between these two networks and connected them to form the largest public telecommunications network in the world, excluding the telephone system. Western Union also renamed the TWX service, calling it Telex II.

THE INTERNATIONAL RECORD CARRIERS

An international record carrier (IRC) is an organization that is formally recognized as a provider of international messaging services, and that consequently is able to participate in the revenue sharing arrangements that exist between nations. Although there are many variations of service and structure among the IRCs, there are certain things that are common to all.

Services Provided

The most salient feature of IRCs is the public nature of the communications networks and services they provide. IRCs provide basic communications facilities that are resold to the end user, and that comprise a "public" network in the sense that any person or company may use the service. Although private companies, military organizations, governments and other organizations may have their own dedicated communications channels—often obtained from the same agency or company that provides public services—the existence of a public network, through which any subscriber may be accessed, has been critical to the implementation of generalized electronic mail services. The international public telex network is the most pervasive electronic mail service on earth, transmitting tens of millions of characters each day.*

Criteria for Defining IRCs

There are at least three criteria for defining IRCs. The first is participation in international revenue exchange arrangements for communications services. An IRC is part of an international network that has agreed to pass messages between members and to collect and distribute revenue for the service according to a common formula negotiated between the IRCs.

A second key criterion of an IRC is the ability to establish and issue public telex numbers that can be accessed from anywhere in the world, and that can be used to send messages to telex numbers established by other IRCs, or PTTs.

*In most countries it is possible to go into a particular post office or other designated place and send a telex message to a telex machine or user in the same country or abroad. In the U.S. there are no public telex booths. This function has historically been relegated to Western Union or to other service providers that collect messages and pass them on to an IRC for transmission. Current examples include secretarial agencies providing telex services to clients, over-the-counter service centers for telex messages and interconnection services described in Chapter 9.

A third criterion of an IRC is that the hardware channels used to provide the communications services—the communications switches, computers, and physical wires or lines used by the service subscribers—are owned or controlled by the IRC. In the U.S. this criterion cannot be strictly applied since the lines are controlled, but not owned, by the IRCs. The IRCs lease the physical lines from the telephone company and, with the breakup of AT&T, the local operating companies (LOCs) as well.

In all countries except the U.S., the PTT is responsible for the delivery of the inbound international telegrams (cables). In the U.S., the delivery of these messages is the responsibility of a single IRC: Western Union. Other U.S. IRCs are required to route any cable traffic that is to be delivered as a telegram (hand-delivered hard-copy) through Western Union for delivery.

IRCs IN THE UNITED STATES: MAJORS, MINORS AND PIRATES

Growth of IRCs

For many years, the Western Union Telegraph Co. and AT&T were the only authorized domestic carriers of telecommunications. International Telephone and Telegraph (ITT) and AT&T were responsible for international communications. In 1973 a new communications entrant, Tropical Radio and Telegraph (TRT), challenged the regulatory policy of the FCC and began providing telecommunications services between U.S. clients and the rest of the world.

The basic technique TRT used was to lease high-capacity circuits from other carriers and then collect and ship messages from customers to London, where they were refiled into the international public telex network. Traditional vagaries in rate enforcement have resulted in lower charges to send telex traffic from Britain than from most other countries. As a result, TRT was able to charge less per message than its regulated competitors and still earn a profit. Since then there has been fierce competition between communications carriers and many new forces have entered the fray.

Within a few years, RCA Global communications joined TRT, and then Western Union, in offering international services in competition with ITT. ITT, conversely, became authorized to provide domestic communications services, enabling it to compete directly with the rapidly growing number of communications carriers in the general U.S. domestic market. ITT was the major international record carrier for many years, accounting for 70% to

80% of gross telex revenues. Today ITT also provides communications and operations support by agreement and contract with many nations.

MCI Communications Corp. became a communications giant by challenging the AT&T long distance telephone monopoly. The purchase of Western Union International (WUI) in 1982 provided MCI with an instant IRC license and an international presence.

Major and Minor Carriers

In the attempt to keep up with a rapidly evolving technological milieu and the pressures of U.S. enterprise, the FCC has adopted a policy of authorizing multiple IRCs to compete in the international arena. The FCC defines two categories of IRC, major and minor. A major carrier has at least 7% of the total market share; a minor carrier has less than that in market share. As of early 1984 the major carriers were ITT, Western Union, RCA, TRT and MCI. The minor carriers were Graphnet, FTCC and CCI.

The regulated tariff (the price the IRC is allowed to charge the public) is higher for the major IRCs than for the minor ones. This difference is intended to provide a competitive advantage to the minor player and lower costs to new or innovative users. It is unclear how long this two-tiered structure will last, since the competition is intense and telecommunications technology is changing more quickly than regulatory structures can be revised.

Pirates

Virtually any company that wishes to apply for carrier authorization can do so and, if the application and services are adequate, can become an authorized IRC, albeit a minor one. Some communications companies don't even bother with the authorization process. A company that provides international communications services in competition with authorized IRCs, but does not adhere to standard tariffs or to service conventions, is often called a "pirate" or, more neutrally, an alternate carrier.

The alternate carrier can provide some low-cost services but, not being a formal, authorized carrier, it often does not have a full range of service for the customer. An alternate carrier must still have communication with the authorized carriers to enable users to send, for example, cables or telex messages to other users of the public network. Many of the alternate carriers operate on such a narrow profit margin that they have been unable to endure price wars with authorized carriers or other pirates, and have disappeared or changed ownership, management or both. This has undoubtedly contributed to the pirate image of alternate carriers. However, there are companies that provide reliable and stable services for their customers, while operating completely out of the authorized international tariff and service standards.

CHOICES AND RECOMMENDATIONS

Ultimately a selection must be made from the many choices available in the communications market. As with most things, there is no single answer that is always right. Most IRCs provide similar services, although there is evidence that not every IRC will be able to provide all of the services that are being developed and tested. The very large and sophisticated IRCs provide a broad range of service and flexibility; yet, in some cases, the very size of the IRC is an impediment to the effective solution of a particular communications problem. Smaller IRCs or alternate carriers may fulfill the requirements for particular applications, but often don't have a full range of service and support for the customer as needs change.

Heavy Usage

For a user spending more than a few hundred dollars a month, the selection of an IRC will often be based as much on value-added and support services as on cost. Large corporations may select an IRC on the basis of special criteria such as provision of private, dedicated circuits and high-speed broadband communications capabilities. Many companies use several IRCs and alternate carriers for different kinds of messages or different applications.

Lighter Usage

Small users with less than a few hundred dollars a month of international communications are often cost-conscious and reluctant to select an IRC based on the value-added services that are available. At all sizes and levels, however, the competition for the user's communications dollar is intense and the choices varied.

Most recently, some electronic mail services, software packages and special interconnection services have begun to provide users with the capability of sending or receiving messages from one or more IRC networks through the EMS system. These services effectively select the IRC for the user as an adjunct or by-product of other choices. (Some of these services are covered in more detail in Chapters 4, 8 and 9.)

COSTS OF TELEX AND TWX SERVICES

The costs of telex and TWX services are often complex and may contain obscure elements which make it difficult to compare carriers, in spite of the fact that these costs are supposedly regulated by FCC tariff in the United States. Users should be aware that although the rates for basic telex service are regulated, there are many optional and value-added services that are priced separately and may differ from one carrier to another.

Factors Influencing Telex and TWX Pricing

One of the variables affecting the telex costs incurred by the user is the type of access that is employed. The traditional method of accessing telex services is through a dedicated telex line, which runs directly into a company's premises from a local or regional operations center. These lines are actually provided by the local telephone company. Depending upon the location of the company site, the costs for these lines will vary. An organization may typically assume line costs will be between $35 and $80 per month; more expensive prices will apply in outlying and rural areas.

Once a user has a telex line, the next variable encountered is the price of the terminal that will be connected to that line and dedicated to the telex application. While it is not legal to provide free terminals to telex customers, the carriers can often provide a selection of terminal equipment at very reasonable rental rates, and sometimes provide free paper, ribbons or other supplies.

Standard Cost of Domestic Telex and TWX

Once the user has a line and terminal, and has paid installation costs ranging from $150 to $300 or more, it is possible to start sending telex messages. As of early 1984, the normal domestic rate for sending a telex message from one carrier's number to a telex number provided by a different carrier (for example, from ITT to Western Union) was $.4775 per minute. If the message is destined for a telex number issued by the same carrier, the rate may be as low as $.3475 per minute. (These are flat rates, excluding monthly line charges.)

Standard Western Union telex rates are higher: $.4518 per minute for telex calls and $.5146 for use of the TWX network (again, excluding line charges). However, because the TWX network operates at a higher speed than telex (10 characters per second, as opposed to approximately six characters per second on the telex network), the transmission time for a TWX message is less than for a telex message. This makes the actual cost per message very similar between the two networks. There is a one-minute minimum on TWX calls with subsequent minutes measured and charged to the next 1/10 minute increment.

The measure for both networks is based upon a standard telex minute. Under ideal circumstances, the telex network will enable the transmission rate of 6.6 characters per second, or 396 characters per minute. The call is measured based upon the elapsed time between the first exchange of answerbacks at the initiation of the call to the final exchange of answerbacks at the termination of that call.

Standard Cost of International Telex

As described elsewhere in this chapter, the rates for international telex are established between countries through a complex structure of committees and working groups. For U.S. users these rates are established and regulated by the FCC. The rates vary from country to country, with more than 35 different tariffed prices for international telex currently operative. These range from $.31 per minute from the U.S. to Canada to $2.54 per minute to, for example, the United Arab Emirates (UAE).

Users are also charged a domestic component for their international calls. A one minute call from an ITT telex machine to the UAE would cost $.38 (domestic component) plus $2.54 (international component) for a total of $2.92. The Canadian call would cost $.69. For a Western Union telex user, the call to the UAE would cost $.45 (domestic component) plus $2.54 for a total of $2.99. Minor IRCs are allowed to charge about 10% less for the same call.

Another cost factor for international telex is that for many countries there is a minimum charge of three minutes per call, regardless of actual transmission time.

Other Factors Affecting Telex Costs

If a user chooses not to use a dedicated line and terminal for telex services, additional variables may apply. Most carriers provide a DDD access option that enables the customer to dial into the telex network using an ASCII terminal, and to communicate at higher speeds with the telex service. Even though messages are transmitted at a higher speed, they will still be charged for based on the standard telex minute described above; i.e. as if transmission were taking place at 6.6 characters per second.

Some carriers offer enhanced telex access service, which makes store-and-forward and stored address facilities available to the user. The carrier may charge higher rates for such a service, even if a particular user doesn't take advantage of all of the capabilities. In some cases there may be extra fees for confirmation notices, or for the ability to access the system from a local or toll-free telephone number.

Guidelines for Comparing Telex Costs

Because of the variations in the pricing of telex service from one carrier to another, it is often easier to use a general rule of thumb for comparing communications costs then to attempt to provide exact estimates. For users equipped with a dedicated line and terminal, standard telex costs (excluding line charges) will be approximately $.40 to $.50 per minute for domestic calls. If the higher speed DDD access mode or optional services such as store-and-forward capability are used, costs will be $.10 to $.20 per minute higher. In addition to these domestic components, the current applicable international cost component must be included for communications outside the U.S.

Competition Among Carriers

The communications field has become extremely competitive in recent years with the advent of deregulation and the introduction of new technologies. Carriers are competing not only against each other but also against the alternate or pirate carriers that operate outside of FCC tariffs and charge 20% to 30% less than IRCs for certain lucrative traffic without having to provide a complete range of service. In order to compete with the pirates, carriers are constantly establishing short-term tariffs (through a filing with the FCC) that offer users substantial discounts under special circumstances.

Examples of special discounts include seasonal promotions, designed to be effective for limited periods of time, and prepayment discounts wherein users buy a number of telex minutes ahead of time for a special rate. Other promotional techniques include premium gift offerings to customers that meet or exceed various billing thresholds. Given the current competitive market for telex services, it pays users to shop around for the best deal from the various carriers.

INTERNATIONAL REGULATORY AGENCIES

In the international arena, there are several different organizations that are active in the regulation of international telecommunications. These organizations do not always work in concert with each other and, in any case, none of the regulations, conventions or decisions is legally binding. Furthermore, the various policies adopted by these international groups often fail to consider certain categories of service or technology: for example, there is no international agreement covering dedicated leased circuits. Each country derives and implements its own policies and powers with respect to the availability and accessibility of private communications circuits. (When one stops to consider the enormous barriers and bureaucracies that must be overcome and coordinated, it is surprising that international telecommunications succeed at all!)

Despite these shortcomings, the agencies do provide some regulatory framework for international telecommunications. The structure of several major international agencies is discussed below.

The International Telecommunications Union (ITU)

The ITU is the senior policy-making agency for telecommunications between nations. It was formed in 1865 as the International Telegraph Union. In 1948 it acquired formal status as a specialized agency of the United Nations. The ITU attempts to coordinate international communications through various policy-making units.

The Plenipotentiary Conference is the main controlling body of the Union, responsible for statement of basic policy in the International Telecommunications Convention. The Plenipotentiary Conference also elects a 29-member Administrative Council which controls the union between conferences. A second policy-making unit of the ITU is the Administrative Conference, which can be either a world or a regional conference. The Administrative Conferences are charged with the continuing revision of telegraph regulations, telephone regulations, radio regulations and additional radio regulations.

The Administrative Council, in addition to controlling the ITU's finances and staffing, is also responsible for the implementation, among member nations, of the conventions, the regulations and the decisions of the major conferences. Four permanent organs are controlled by the Administrative Council: the General Secretariat, the International Frequency Regulation Board (IFRB), the International Radio Consultative Committee (CCIR) and the International Telephone and Telegraph Consultative Committee (CCITT), which makes studies and issues recommendations with respect to technical and operating questions in the area of telegraph and telephone communications.

Of these, the CCITT is the one most frequently involved in establishment of standards and regulations which affect the use of the electronic mail service described in this book.

Commonwealth Telecommunications Council

Until the end of World War II, Great Britain and its territories were linked with an electronic mail network, in the form of submarine cables and high-frequency (HF) radio facilities, owned and operated by a private British firm, Cable and Wireless Ltd. When the British Government nationalized its international record carriers in 1946, Cable and Wireless became a government monopoly and a series of agreements was implemented that nationalized the operating companies in Canada, Australia, India, South Africa and Ceylon. The Commonwealth Telecommunications Board was established to coordinate operations and rates among these countries. This structure was later changed to the Commonwealth Telecommunications Council to accommodate membership by any of the 32 old and new Commonwealth nations.

CEPT

The Conference Europeene des Administrations des Postes et des Telecommunications (CEPT) was formed in 1959 to regulate postal revenue agreements in Europe. The CEPT coordinates much telecommunications policy in Europe, but it is a secretive body without the general participation of user communities. Some observers believe that the CEPT's main focus is on maintaining the complete monopoly of access to telecommunications services enjoyed by the PTTs.

Latin American Organizations

There are three regional organizations attempting to coordinate the chaotic Latin American telecommunications picture. The Conferencia InterAmericana de Telecommunicaciones is a small organization within the Organization of American States. The Central American Telecommunications Conference (COMTELCA) has five members (Costa Rica, El Salvador, Guatemala, Honduras and Nicaragua) and attempts to coordinate communication between Central America and the rest of the world. El Grupo Regional Andino comprises Bolivia, Colombia, Chile, Ecuador, Peru and Venezuela, all of which have agreed to integrate their facilities into a combined Andean Regional Network.

SUMMARY

IRCs or alternate carriers are an integral component of any electronic mail application requiring international communications. The IRCs are developing new technologies for electronic communications, and are introducing new services, such as electronic mail services and special software packages, described in later chapters. However, while TWX (Telex II) and basic telex service are rapidly being replaced by more sophisticated systems in the U.S., internationally, telex service will continue to be the most widespread form of electronic mail throughout this decade.

4

Computer-Based Message Systems

As we have seen from the preceding chapter, the first generation of electronic mail goes back to the early part of this century in the form of teletype machines. The next generation evolved much more recently, in parallel with development of the computer technology that makes possible electronic mail as we know it today. This next generation is the computer-based message system, or CBMS, the type of system that is most commonly associated with the term "electronic mail."

A CBMS is an electronic mail system that incorporates word processing capabilities and (usually) file management capabilities for storage and retrieval of information into one *centralized* system. Generally speaking, one large computer acts as the "host" for the system, and users of the mail system must access that host computer in order to send or receive mail. This centralization to a single host facility means that a number of functions, including long-term storage, rerouting and multiple addressing of messages, can be handled effectively.

The two primary options for implementing a CBMS are 1.) installing a software package on a local or private computer system (usually a mainframe or large minicomputer rather than a microcomputer) and 2.) accessing a remote network or information utility. To get some background on the differences between these two options, let's take a look at the way in which CBMS developed.

THE DEVELOPMENT OF CBMS

In the early days of computing, data communication was not an integral part of computer systems. Information was fed into computers via cards onto which the instructions for running programs had been key-punched. Second generation computers offered remote access capability; that is, terminals were connected to the computer so that instructions could be keyed directly into it. Although these terminals might be removed from the immediate vicinity of the computer, perhaps into another part of the same building, they were generally wired to the computer by means of a permanent connection, so that each terminal had its own direct line into the computer. This type of data communications design is referred to as "hard-wired."

Early Computer Messaging Systems

The first computer messaging systems were probably devised to allow a computer operator to send a message to another operator at a terminal—perhaps to say that the computer would be unavailable at a certain hour, or that a particular system problem had been fixed. Because the computer could be used to store information, such messages could be created and directed to particular users even when they weren't actually accessing the computer, so that the information would be available the next time they logged on. This rudimentary capability to store a message for pick-up at some later time by the recipient is the basis upon which all CBMSs were developed.

In-house CBMS

In this way, many organizations with existing computer facilities developed their own in-house or private electronic mail systems. Messaging quickly became a two-way activity, with the users developing ways to send messages back to the operator, and then to each other, using the existing in-house computer network.

Direct Access

Figure 4.1 illustrates the configuration of such a rudimentary electronic mail system. In this configuration, each terminal is connected directly to the central computer via internal data communications lines. When terminals are hard-wired to the central computer, each terminal has its own "port" or direct access point into the computer. This means that the user need only turn on the terminal in order to be connected to the host system; there is no need to dial-up a port for access to the computer.

This mode of connection works very well for a relatively small user population. However, dedicating one port to each user can become more difficult as the user population grows, because it can become very expensive to provide a full-time access port to each user. Further, unlike programmers or other users who require constant access to the computer, electronic mail users don't really need to have a constant access to the system. Rather, each individual is likely to do a brief mail check several times a day.

Figure 4.1: Direct Access Configuration

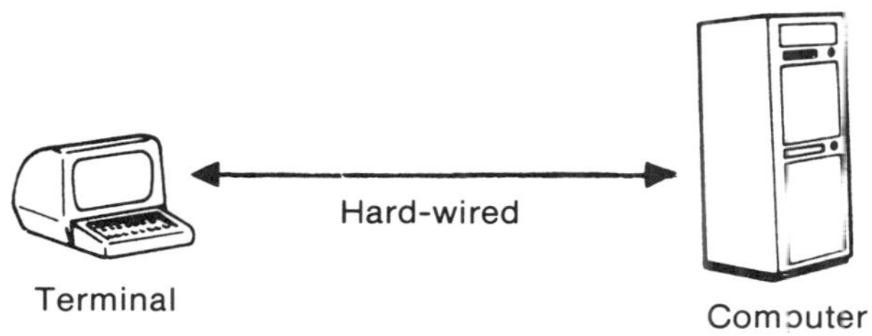

Dial-up Access

Therefore, even for access to an in-house communications network, it may be most efficient to provide dial-up access, rather than direct access, to the computer for most users. Figure 4.2 shows this form of access.

Figure 4.2: Dial-up Access Configuration

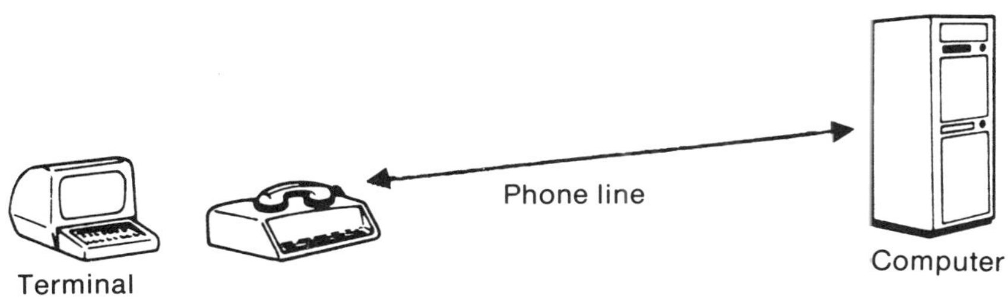

In the dial-up mode of access, each terminal is equipped with a telephone and modem or acoustic coupler (see Technical Note 4:1). In order to make a connection to the computer, the user must dial a phone number to access a port. A configuration of this type generally does not have enough ports for every user to be connected at the same time; thus, in peak usage times all ports may be busy. In general, however, users will be accessing the system at different times so that the load will be equalized.

For most organizations, installation of a central computer facility cannot be justified solely on the basis of EMS capabilities. However, with many computer installations, the general operating system software includes some form of electronic mail capability as part of the standard package. Thus, if the organization already has a computer facility, the capability to send

> Technical Note 4:1
>
> A modem is a device that allows digitally coded data to be transmitted over phone lines. Regular phone lines are designed to transmit sounds rather than electronic pulses. The modem takes the electronic pulses generated by the computer and transforms them into sound waves that can be carried over a phone line. This process involves the "modulation" of the electronic pulse into a sound wave at the sending end and the "demodulation" of the sound back into an electronic pulse at the receiving end. Thus, a MOdulator/DEModulator is a *modem*. Some modems transmit the signal through the telephone handset. These are called acoustic couplers.

messages within the organization may indeed exist, making it possible to create an electronic mail network by providing terminal access to users. If an in-house computer system does not have this capability, then purchase and installation of a CBMS software package may be a cost-effective way to obtain EMS functions within the organization. Interorganizational communication, however, is not possible with such a configuration.

Organizations that have in-house CBMS services employ a variety of telecommunications options to provide the transmission link to the host computer. These include dedicated leased lines (a line or a circuit allocated by AT&T specifically for the organization's use) and, in the case of some geographically dispersed organizations, satellite networks. However, only organizations that have a very high volume of data transmission can generally justify the cost of such a system. Further, increasing numbers of organizations want to be able to use EMS to communicate externally, with other companies. These and other factors have led to the growth of commercial CBMS services.

Commercial CBMS

Today's computers permit mass storage and interactive retrieval over long distance communications networks. The evolution of these networks, the capability to handle large numbers of users on large host computer facilities and the standardization of data transmission to ASCII code have all contributed to the development of commercial computer-based message systems. These systems offer the opportunity to purchase the use of computer services, spreading the cost over a large number of users. It is possible to obtain access to one of these services by dialing into the host computer using an inexpensive computer terminal; this eliminates the need to maintain a local computer facility. Figure 4.3 illustrates the components of a CBMS in which a commercial service bureau provides the computer power.

Figure 4.3: Commercial CBMS Configuration

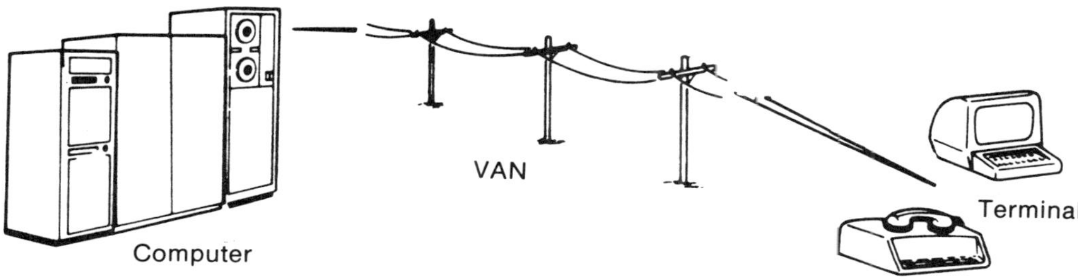

Value Added Networks

The primary difference between a private CBMS and a commercial system is the use of a data communications network—such as Tymnet, Telenet or Uninet—to access the host computer. These networks are the most commonly used option for long-distance data transmission, because they are designed specifically for *data*, not voice, transmission. By employing high-speed, high-volume lines connecting major population centers, these networks can achieve economies of scale for long-distance communication that allow them to offer pricing which is very competitive with regular long-distance DDD rates from AT&T.

In addition, since these networks don't have to handle voice transmission, they are able to employ technologies which reduce the amount of noise and interference on the lines, resulting in fewer errors in transmission (see Technical Note 4:2). Because the networks provide additional services for error correction and control of data transmission, they are also called "value added networks" or "VANs."

The VANs use a fee structure based primarily on connect time to the network, quite independent of the location of the host computer(s) accessed in the particular session. Therefore, it makes no difference where the computer to which you are connected is located—telecommunications charges will be based on the number of minutes and, in some cases, the

> Technical Note 4:2
>
> The value added networks employ a technology known as "packet switching" to transmit data from one point to another. A particular file or message will be separated into smaller packets of uniform length, and each packet sent separately through the network. The individual parts are then reassembled when all reach the destination. This splitting up of messages allows each bit of data to be sent through the network via the least congested route, for optimization of the available transmission capacity. The routing of these packets is handled by computers acting as network controllers.

number of characters transmitted. This is quite a contrast to the mode of charging for regular long-distance telephone calls, where the distance involved does determine charges. Depending on your location, however, it may be necessary to make a long-distance call in order to connect into the network.

The three major value added networks are based in different parts of the country and each has its own network configuration serving slightly different geographic areas. Currently, all three serve the major metropolitan areas, and all are expanding network access to include an increasing number of smaller population centers. Price and service capabilities are similar for all three, although Uninet is the newest one and currently provides access to somewhat fewer host computers and is somewhat less expensive. The determining criteria for choosing a network will be that it provide access to the host system of choice and that it has a nearby node which can be reached through a local phone call. Rural areas are not yet served comprehensively by these networks, which may result in increased costs for long-distance phone calls just to get into the communications network.

ADVANTAGES OF COMMERCIAL CBMS SERVICES

Centralized Message Control

As noted previously, the characteristic which most distinguishes a CBMS from other types of electronic mail is the centralized receipt and transmission of messages. As illustrated above, each user communicates with the host computer, not directly with other users in the system. The computer provides a mailbox for each user, in which incoming messages are stored. It is not necessary for a user to be connected to the system in order to be the recipient of a message. New messages are just deposited and stored in that mailbox and are available to be read the next time the user accesses the system.

There are a number of advantages to this type of centralization. First, it allows message senders and recipients to work independently of each other. Consider the problems of the early teletype networks, in which users transmitted messages directly from one teletype machine to another via a real-time connection. For a teletype message to be transmitted, the recipient's terminal had to respond to the call and print out the message. If it were already receiving another message, or being used to compose text, the incoming message could not be received.

As the number of participants in a message network increases, the frequency of this type of interference also increases. With a CBMS, however, the message sender need make contact only with the host computer. If the message recipient is sending or receiving a message, or tying up the terminal in some other way, it does not prevent someone else in the network from sending a message.

Because it eliminates the need for direct connection from user to user, a CBMS can efficiently serve a large user population. However, this centralization does require a very high degree of reliability from the host computer, since the entire network is paralyzed if the host is not available.

Second, centralized storage of messages permits more efficient message handling. Although messages are received by the host computer intermittently over a period of time, the recipient sees all new messages at once, each time the mail is checked. The batching of messages allows the recipient to respond according to priorities. Messages can be transmitted to others during the same online session in which messages are received.

Distance-independent Costs

Using a central computer as a message system host also means that the location of the recipient does not affect the cost of message transmission. This is because the message is actually being transmitted to the host computer, not to the recipient. In fact, the location of the host computer—be it New York, Ohio or California—is also immaterial to cost, owing to the fee structures of the value added networks.

Because of this distance-independent charging mechanism, a CBMS is well suited to an environment where the participants in a message network are separated by significant distances. It is possible to estimate costs on the basis of the volume of the message traffic, without having to worry about the configuration of the message traffic in terms of the location of various participants. Of even greater importance is the fact that, once a message is stored in the host computer, it is available immediately, whether the recipient is in the next room, across the country or even on another continent.

Equipment Compatibility

In a typical CBMS installation, the host computer does all the work. The terminals that are used to access the system have no capabilities other than providing a keyboard to enter data and a printer or other display device to show what is being sent or received. These "dumb" terminals are just extensions of the host computer, providing no functions when not connected to it. Therefore, all text creation and revision, all storage of messages and all message manipulation is done online while connected to the host; nothing is done while offline. Because only a standard terminal is required, a CBMS can often be installed using equipment that is already available.

The value added networks also serve a function in this capacity, since there are many different devices that can be used as computer terminals. Although the ASCII format is the widely used standard for communications, there are still differences in the way the standard is implemented in terms of communications features such as duplex, parity and baud rate (see Technical Note 4:3).

Technical Note 4:3

The terms "half duplex" and "full duplex" are used to designate whether or not the host computer echoes back each character that is sent from the terminal. In a half duplex system, the host computer does not echo back, and the character typed at the keyboard is displayed as it is typed. With full duplex, each character is echoed, and displayed after being echoed by the host. When a full duplex system is accessed by a terminal configured for half duplex, each character appears twice—once as typed, and once when echoed. The VAN can correct this by suppressing display of the echoed character.

The value added networks provide the necessary protocol translations to enable terminals of almost any type to communicate with the host computer. This enables the implementation of a message network using whatever equipment is available in a particular location, so that it is not necessary to install uniform equipment at every site. This means that it is possible to use the facilities of a CBMS to allow incompatible pieces of equipment to communicate with each other.

COMMERCIAL CBMS FEATURES

Using the EMS services of a commercial computer system is an easy and relatively inexpensive way to implement an electronic mail system. There is also a good selection of vendors from which to choose. The six major ones are: OnTyme, a service of Tymshare (the Tymnet telecommunications network is a subsidiary of Tymshare); Telemail, a service of GTE Telenet; Dialcom, a subsidiary of ITT; MCI Mail, a service of MCI Corp.; and the mail systems of the two best known information utilities—CompuServe and The Source.

General Electric Information Service Co. (GEISCO) offers the Quikcom service, which has been available only to users of other GEISCO services. In mid-1984, GEISCO announced that Quikcom will be offered as a public access communications service.

These services have varying system features and capabilities. Most do not have all the capabilities listed below, and some make available features not mentioned here. The capabilities discussed below will provide a basic "shopping list" to aid in the evaluation of the different systems. The six major EMS systems are described and compared in the next section.

Online Text Editing

Any CBMS allows the user to key in the text of messages while online. In most systems, the edit mode is "line-by-line." In order to revise text, you must identify the line that needs revision, display that particular line, and insert, delete, or change a string of characters. This type of text editing works reasonably well for the brief messages that make up the bulk of most EMS traffic. However, it can be a tedious process if a large amount of revision needs to be done on lengthy text or complete documents.

Some systems offer "screen-by-screen" editing, in which it is possible to move a cursor around a terminal display screen to make corrections. For the most part, these more sophisticated text display features are available only on in-house systems, where dedicated communications lines can be used to provide the necessary high-speed transmission to send and format a full screen of data at a time. If a remote, commercial system with line-by-line editing is being used, it may be best to use some other text editing device to prepare and manipulate text prior to transmission.

Message Handling

What happens to a message after it is read by the recipient? An important feature to evaluate in a CBMS is the way in which messages can be handled and tracked after transmission and after receipt. For example, a CBMS should allow the user to forward a message to another recipient after reading it. It should be possible to review a list of all messages received from a particular person, all messages sent in a particular time period, all messages sent but not yet read, and a list showing when each particular message was received. Capabilities such as these reduce the time spent in finding out the status of a particular query or request.

A CBMS service generally allows the user to address a message to more than one recipient. One way to do this is to list the names of the multiple recipients each time a message is sent. However, a more sophisticated system will allow the user to create mailing lists or distribution lists that can be permanently stored and reused as needed.

These rudimentary record management capabilities are critical in increasing the efficiency with which messages and information can be received and handled. A CBMS can support these functions in an integrated fashion, presenting the user with a simple set of commands to use in forwarding and distributing information. Therefore, this type of system has excellent potential for easy integration into all levels of business communication.

Message Storage and Retrieval

In addition to message handling and temporary storage, a CBMS may also provide long-term storage capability, offering the user the opportunity to create an online database of messages. This online storage capability has the potential to replace paper files. However, in order to be effective, online storage must be coupled with adequate message retrieval capability.

Message retrieval capabilities vary widely among commercial CBMS services. The most commonly available retrieval point is by the message number assigned to a given message when it is created. In addition, the system should support retrieval by name of sender and recipient of message, by date sent and by one or two subject categories. These retrieval points represent the most common classifications in a manual filing system.

In a very sophisticated system, more advanced indexing of stored messages is available. Methods range from indexing of all significant words describing the subject of the memo, to retrieval on additional key words from the text, to full-text indexing. The last level of retrieval is not necessary for most message filing systems.

Message Formatting

Much of the information that is passed through an office is formatted in very specific ways—purchase orders, invoices, sales reports and other statistics are just a few examples of formatted data. Transmitting these into an electronic medium requires a system that has the capability to store such forms and present a particular form to the user to be completed online as needed. Every business has its own range of required forms and its own information requirements. Therefore, the CBMS should allow users to easily design and set up formats to meet local needs, and should not impose rigid formats.

In order to prepare forms, users will almost certainly need far more programming knowledge than they would just to use the system for messaging activities. In general, the more sophisticated the forms capability is, the more complex the programming required for setup will be. Use of sophisticated forms capability will usually work best if forms are created only by a designated CBMS administrator or service coordinator within the organization.

Computer Conferencing

The capability to send a message to multiple recipients at the same time can be expanded to support online communication among a particular group of people, or computer conferencing. (A conference, in this sense, is a group of mail users who have a common area of interest about which they wish to share information.) In computer conferencing, the CBMS supports the creation of a centralized file, into which a description of the topic of the conference can be placed. The members of the conference can not only review the contents of this file, but they can also add comments, be notified of new contributions to the file and exchange information with the other conference participants.

It is important to note that this kind of conferencing is not "real-time" communication. Of course, one of the advantages of a CBMS is that users need *not* be online simultaneously. However, some CBMS services also allow users who do happen to be online at the same time to send messages to each other in real-time. Although useful for quick or urgent messages, this type of real-time communication is not very practical for most messaging applications, since it takes a relatively long time for text to be keyed in online, compared to the speed with which the recipient can read it. It is therefore too time consuming for lengthy messages.

MAJOR CBMS SERVICES

The six electronic mail systems described below are run on central computer systems and made available to subscribers. Each offers the basic mail capabilities described at the beginning of this chapter; each also has its own special characteristics. Table 4.1 compares the features, capabilities and charges. It can also be used as a checklist for evaluating the systems. All prices are as of early 1984 and should be used for comparison only.

There are numerous electronic mail software packages which can be purchased and mounted on an in-house computer system to provide similar support for an organization's internal messaging requirements. (Addresses and telephone numbers for these and other suppliers can be found in Appendix B.)

InfoPlex

InfoPlex, offered by CompuServe, is a command-driven, full service electronic mail system oriented toward the business community. Business support features include the capability of creating prompted forms, detailed message traffic reports, system security, transaction-based pricing and computer-assisted training. Connection to E-COM for delivery of first class mail is available, as well as access to other CompuServe information services.

Although InfoPlex is designed for the business market, CompuServe also makes available another electronic mail service via its nighttime information utility service. Known as EMAIL, this service is available from 6 p.m. to 5 a.m. on weeknights, and all day during the weekend. At $5.00 per hour, this service is a great bargain. Its off-hours availability and relatively unsophisticated system features make it most appropriate for personal rather than business use. The listings for CompuServe on the comparison chart describe InfoPlex, not EMAIL.

The service is available through the CompuServe's network ComLink, as well as through Tymnet.

Dialcom

Dialcom, a service of ITT, is a prompted system which provides a full range of message handling and file retrieval capabilities. In addition to basic electronic mail, it offers bulletin boards, computer conferencing and terminal-to-terminal chatting. Dialcom provides gateways to other communications services, so that messages created on the system can be delivered to telex terminals, as mailgrams or telegrams, or sent through the U.S. E-COM system.

In addition to communications services, Dialcom offers a number of other information services. These include access to stock information, the UPI newswire, the Official Airline Guide and the ABI/Inform business information file. Management support services are also available.

The system is available through direct dial, Tymnet and Telenet.

MCI Mail

MCI Mail, introduced as the "nation's new postal system" in fall 1983, is distinguished by the provision of a wide variety of delivery options. In addition to electronic delivery to another MCI mailbox, an MCI message can be printed on letter-quality stationery and sent to any street address. Delivery can be through the regular first class mail, or guaranteed for overnight or same day arrival. Cost ranges from $1.00 for electronic delivery to $25.00 for same day delivery.

When introduced, the system was available only in "basic" mode, which provides minimal online storage and message handling capabilities. An

Table 4.1: CBMS System Comparison

System Feature	InfoPlex	Dialcom	MCI Mail	OnTyme	Source Mail	Telemail
Messaging						
Memo header (date, sender, etc.)	X	X	X	X	X	X
Subject heading	X	X	X		X	X
Multiple recipients	X	X	X	X	X	X
Message forwarding	X	X		X	X	X
Message cancelling	X			X		X
Message acknowledgement	X	X		X	X	X
List incoming mail	X	X	X	X	X	X
List outgoing mail				X		
Save received or sent mail	X	X		X	X	X
File Storage						
Private storage	X	X		X	X	X
Shared (designated access)	X	X		X	X	X
Public (unrestricted access)	X			X		
Stored message/file retrieval						
By date		X			X	X
By sender		X			X	X
By subject		X		X	X	X
By system access number	X	X		X	X	X
Bulletin Board						
Read only	X					X
Read/write		X		X	X	
Conferencing						
Online chatting		X			X	
Public conference		X			X	
Private conference		X			X	

Table 4.1: CBMS System Comparison (cont.)

System Feature	InfoPlex	Dialcom	MCI Mail	OnTyme	SourceMail	Telemail
Text Manipulation						
Line editor	X	X	X	X	X	X
Formatting (paging, etc.)				X	X	
Full screen editing						
Spelling error detection		X			X	
User Aids						
Menus/command prompting		X	X	opt	opt	X
Online help instructions	X	X	X	X	X	X
User defined forms	X			X	X	X
Delivery Options						
To mailbox on system	X	X	X	X	X	X
Outdial to user terminal				X	X	X
First class mail	X	X	X		X	
Mailgram		X	X	X	X	
Same day courier			X			
Connection to TWX/telex		X	X	X		X
Service Charges						
Start-up	$500.00	-	-	-	$100.00	-
Monthly minimum	500.00	$100.00	-	$500.00	10.00	$ 5.00
Monthly service fee	-	-	-	200.00	-	140.00
Per connect hour (prime)	-	18.00	-	3.00	20.75	14.00
Per connect hour (nonprime)	-	11.00	-	3.00	7.75	7.00
Per 1000 characters transmitted	-	-	-	.25	-	-
Per message transmitted	.35	-	$1.00	-	-	-
Per file/form edited	.45	-	-	-	-	-
Per character stored/saved	.02/600	.40/block		.01/1000		.05/1000

advanced version, which provides added storage capability and the ability to create distribution lists and forward messages, is to be available in 1984. Entries for MCI on the comparison chart show the capabilities of the basic version.

The system is available through the MCI communications network.

OnTyme II

The Tymshare service OnTyme is a command-driven system which provides excellent message tracking and filing features. In addition to messaging services, the system offers a "load" command that can be used to transfer documents between non-compatible word processors. The capability of sending messages to telex and TWX destinations is available through an interconnection service.

Using English language commands, users can easily program command execution routines into the system. This capability, which can be used to develop prompted versions of the system to the specifications of the individual user, was added in 1983.

OnTyme is accessed through the Tymnet communications network.

SourceMail

SourceMail, offered by Source Telecomputing Corp., is available in either a menu-driven or command version, which can be chosen at the option of the user. In addition to electronic mail, The Source provides access to online chatting and computer conferencing and can be used to send a Western Union mailgram. System use charges are hourly, with low rates available for evening and weekend use. Higher rates apply to 1200 baud access.

These communications services are options within the menu of service available on The Source. They include news and business information, games, software and program execution, travel reservations, electronic typesetting transmission and more. Some of these services are SOURCE*PLUS and are available at extra charge.

The Source can be accessed by direct dial, in-WATS, Tymnet and Telenet.

Telemail

GTE Telenet's Telemail is a prompted system. With Telemail, an organization can create its own hierarchies or subsets of communicating groups, to provide a structure for the flow of electronic mail messages. For example, sales and customer service departments could be designated as separate groups at the same level in a hierarchy, and subsets of each one (for example, regional offices) could be defined as well. Message transmission would always be possible within each subset, but may or may not be allowed between groups, depending on how the organization decides to set it up. Telenet also provides the capability for creating bulletin boards at each branch point in the hierarchy and for displaying directories of all users with particular subsets or groups of subsets.

Telemail provides a sophisticated software facility to support the creation of locally defined message formats, which is done at the level of the system administrator for a particular organization.

The system is accessed through the Telenet communications network.

SUMMARY

We have seen that CBMS functions evolved with the development of remote entry computer systems. CBMS software can be installed on an in-house computer system that has its own data transmission system or accessed through a commercial service utility.

In a CBMS, messages are stored in the central computer for retrieval at the convenience of the recipient. Access is usually through the public data communications networks, making costs distance-independent. Many types of terminal and other equipment can be used to access these systems. Although system features vary, most CBMSs offer online text editing, message tracking and file storage. Some also offer advanced services such as computer conferencing and prompted message formats.

It is important to remember that with a CBMS, all message processing and all of the control of the system is done by a remote computer host—in other words, all of the intelligence of the system is centralized. In the next chapter, we will examine the use of intelligent hardware to provide local or distributed processing of messages.

5

Distributed Electronic Mail Networks

The development of microprocessor technology in the last five years has had a dramatic impact on the design and delivery of messaging systems. The early public teletype network represented a relatively primitive form of message handling, since there was no capability to store and process messages—i.e., no intelligence—in the system. More sophisticated message handling capabilities are provided by computer-based message systems, but the intelligence of the system is still centralized—in the host computer, rather than at each individual terminal or workstation.

GROWTH OF LOCAL CONTROL

Development of Intelligent Equipment

The emergence of the microprocessor or "computer on a chip," and the resultant miniaturization of computer memory, has led to the development of a completely new generation of intelligent equipment. Although the microcomputer is the most widely known type of equipment using microprocessor technology, there are many others. Intelligent terminals, smart modems and other kinds of communications equipment all perform their specialized functions through the use of microprocessors. This technology has allowed the transfer of computing and communications operations from host computer systems to the local workstation. A communications system in which each workstation is equipped to provide message handling functions is the basic operating unit of a local or distributed messaging network.

Shift Toward Distributed Processing

The growth of distributed processing has spurred the development of many alternatives beyond TWX/telex or a CBMS. In some cases, the new equipment has completely replaced these older, but still widely used systems. In other cases, microprocessor-based equipment has been used to enhance and extend these systems, making them more flexible, more powerful, more accessible and less expensive.

This second case, of enhancing previous technology, is by far the more common. The older communications methods are so widely used and accepted throughout the world that it will take many years before they can be completely replaced. In the meantime, many intermediate systems are springing up that will bridge the gap between the past and the future. These microprocessor-based systems are an important alternative for developing a local electronic messaging system.

LOCAL ELECTRONIC MAIL OPTIONS

This chapter will briefly outline the five general types of systems—stand-alone message processing workstations, intelligent peripherals, terminal emulation software, EMS software and communicating word processors—and the communications network options that can be used to link the various locations or nodes of a distributed network. Chapter 7 will examine the hardware-based systems in more detail; Chapter 8 will cover the software alternatives for personal computers and communicating word processors.

Hardware and Software Alternatives

A wide variety of microprocessor-based devices can be used for electronic mail. They range in sophistication from simple auto-dial, auto-answer modems attached to dumb terminals, to custom-built microcomputers with high-volume storage and multiple communications ports. The commercially available systems for distributed message networks listed above can be loosely grouped into two broad categories: those requiring dedicated equipment (stand-alone message processing workstations, intelligent peripherals), in which the communications capabilities are built into the equipment, and those in which general purpose equipment, such as a microcomputer, is tailored for the message function through the use of communications software.

Telecommunications Options

As noted earlier, the main function that distinguishes a distributed system from a centralized system is *local* versus remote control. In distributed systems, the mail functions are provided at each local, intelligent workstation. Because all of the functions are local, much more consideration must be given to data communications protocols than when a single, central remote system is being accessed. (A locally controlled operation also requires somewhat more knowledgeable users, since troubleshooting cannot be referred to a vendor as readily.)

Most microprocessor products are designed to be used in a dial-up environment—that is, on the public telephone network or on an IRC network, not on dedicated networks. For most functions, the sending station operates independently from the receiving station. The public switched networks (DDD phone lines, TWX or telex) are the most common telecommunications channels used to connect the nodes of a distributed network. Protocols for linking into private data networks are also provided by some systems and are needed to develop in-house networks. Most of the transmission will be point-to-point—that is, direct from one user station to another, or to multiple stations on a distribution list.

TYPES OF DISTRIBUTED COMMUNICATIONS SYSTEMS

Stand-alone Message Processing Workstations

The best known of the hardware-based systems are the stand-alone communications processors. These are essentially specially designed, single function microcomputers, with message processing capabilities only. Because they are specifically designed to handle only communications functions, they are generally used in organizations that have a high volume of communications traffic (i.e., incoming or outgoing messages are being handled more than four hours a day).

Such systems are designed to replace the rooms full of telex equipment that were previously used by organizations with heavy communications traffic. They incorporate most, although not all, of the functions of electronic mail. Such systems add many features not available on simple telex machines, reducing costs by improving operator efficiency and providing other sophisticated operations. Examples are the Silent Partner and Micronet, described in Chapter 7.

Intelligent Peripherals

In this type of hardware-based system, the intelligence for handling the messaging functions is built into specialized peripheral equipment. This is usually an enhanced or smart modem (one with local storage, and often message formatting, capability), designed to be used in conjunction with the user's existing word processor, personal computer or standard dumb terminal. Examples of this are the Betacom PCM, DataPort II and Chat II, described in Chapter 7.

These devices are less expensive than the dedicated communications processors, but generally provide less sophisticated functions. An intelligent peripheral can be used to upgrade existing equipment, such as a standard dumb terminal, and allows a single piece of existing equipment to serve additional functions. Generally, such devices are best suited to a low (less than one hour a day) or medium level (one to four hours a day) traffic environment. These systems fall into the category of dedicated equipment, but can be used in conjunction with general purpose terminals.

Terminal Emulation Software for Microcomputers

Almost any microcomputer can be equipped with a communications port and connected to a modem. However, for electronic mail, in addition to a modem, a microcomputer must also be equipped with a software package providing the instructions that will make the micro function as an interactive terminal. Terminal emulation software can cause a microcomputer to emulate either an ASCII terminal, a telex unit or both. With such software, a microcomputer can be used to connect with an external computer or CBMS and, with the appropriate kind of auto-answer modem, can be used to automatically respond to incoming calls and receive the text of messages sent over the communications lines.

Terminal emulation software is just one of many software packages that can be used with a microcomputer station performing a variety of functions. Examples of terminal emulation software packages are Postman and Micro/Telegram, described in Chapter 8.

EMS Software for Microcomputers

More sophisticated microcomputer software packages are available that will provide most of the functions of a full-featured EMS system. Unlike a CBMS, however, the EMS functions of text creation, message store and forwarding, message tracking, etc., are performed at each workstation.

Although such systems operate on off-the-shelf microcomputer hardware, most packages are compatible with only a limited selection of microcomputers and modems. In addition, most of these EMS services can communicate only with other installations equipped with the same hardware and software configuration. Therefore, although these packages provide more functions than a simple terminal emulation package, they are less flexible for wide-scale communication. Examples are Micro/Courier and Transend, described in Chapter 8.

Software for Communicating Word Processors

During the 1970s word processing systems were introduced into many work environments. For many businesses, the introduction of word processing equipment is the first step into office automation. In a 1983 study, International Data Corp. (Framingham, MA) estimated that the installed base for dedicated word processors was 700,000 at year-end 1982, and projected that this would reach 2.6 million units by 1987.[1] Therefore, existing word processing equipment must often be considered in selecting an approach to implementing a communications network.

The basic elements of a word processing station are similar to the basic elements of a computer terminal, with additional capabilities that make each workstation a "smart" terminal. A basic word processing unit consisting of a typewriter-like keyboard for entering text, a display screen, a printer and the capability to store text in a machine-readable format may need only the addition of communications capability to become a node in a distributed message network. The communications function is usually provided by a software package.

At the minimum, individual word processing workstations can often be used as alternative input and receive terminals for electronic mail. Depending on the capabilities of the existing equipment, a well-designed communicating word processor (CWP) can be the basis of a fully featured office automation system integrating the best features of sophisticated document creation and storage with document delivery and message handling.

The software for CWPs is usually provided by the word processing manufacturer. It is typically built into the word processor at the time of purchase, or added on as an enhancement. Examples of communicating word processors are those offered by Wang and NCR, described in Chapter 8.

LINKING DISTRIBUTED NETWORKS INTERNALLY

There are a variety of possibilities for establishing a communications network connecting the intelligent workstations described above. Long-distance communication, or communication between independent organizations, is generally carried out over the public switched networks and these can also be used for in-house communication. However, there are a number of other options for internal communications that may be cost-effective for development of a local electronic communications system.

Direct or Hard Wiring

Most equipment manufacturers will install a communications network to link equipment in-house. Several modes of telecommunication are available to choose from. Each workstation can be connected to the central processor via coaxial cable, twisted wire pair or other local communications link provided by the equipment vendor. The communications protocol is either asynchronous, which is commonly used for dial-up computer communications, or synchronous (see Technical Note 5:1).

Local Area Networks

The local area network (LAN) is a type of communications configuration that is receiving increasing consideration for internal communications among workstations of all types. A LAN is a system for transmitting digital information from one point to two or more others simultaneously, in a relatively small area. Most workstations in a LAN are separated by one or two miles, or less; often, networks are installed completely within one building.

> Technical Note 5:1
>
> In synchronous transmission, data are transmitted in a continuous stream. This transmission requires an intelligent communications handler at each node. When transmission begins, the sending device indicates start of message, and the receiving device prepares for receipt of data. The message is terminated by an end-of-message character from the sending device. In asynchronous transmission, transmission starts as the result of a signal that the previous transmission has been completed. It is characterized by having a fixed or specific frequency of cycles. Asynchronous transmission is best suited to intermittent dial-up communications. Synchronous transmission is well-suited to dedicated communications networks. With synchronous transmission, error-checking bits are not required with every character, and transmission is faster and more reliable than asynchronous.

LANs are usually designed to convey different kinds of traffic: e.g., voice, data, facsimile, video. Therefore, equipment connected to LANs may include CWPs, intelligent terminals, shared disk-storage units, facsimile machines, other peripheral equipment and one or more central processing units. In its simplest format, a LAN may be nothing more than dedicated line or ribbon cable with plug-in connectors for equipment. With a LAN, it is not necessary for each workstation or device to be directly addressed or hard wired to a central processor; this makes it possible for equipment to be moved easily from one location to another without labor-intensive rewiring.

LANs provide much higher-speed communications than regular telephone-based communications, since they are designed to move large amounts of data quickly over short distances far more efficiently than voice-grade phone lines. The two main types of LAN are baseband and broadband, with data transmission speeds ranging from 19,200 bps to 100 million bps (see Technical Note 5:2).

> Technical Note 5:2
>
> The major difference between baseband and broadband LANs is in data capacity. Baseband can carry only one transmission at any moment, while broadband has numerous channels, each of which can carry a separate transmission. Baseband is easy to install and can be moved around, while broadband wiring requires network architecture design that may be built into the building with the other utility support systems. For situations where multiple simultaneous applications are required (for example, hospitals with life support and monitoring sytems, as well as entertainment and data transmission), broadband is appropriate. However, many office networks need the flexibility (portability) of baseband.

Slow Growth of LANs

Despite the obvious advantages offered in terms of speed and capacity, LANs have been fairly slow to be accepted in most office environments. According to International Resource Development (Norwalk, CT), there were approximately 81,000 LAN connections installed by the end of 1982, representing a much smaller number of actual networks. The slow growth has mainly been due to a lack of technical standards, which has made it difficult to install a LAN that will provide easy communication between diverse types of equipment. Instead, most LANs are available only for linking equipment adhering to particular protocol standards. In response to a demand for more open and flexible network design, there has been some movement toward adoption of standards.

Move Toward Standardization

One of the major commercial efforts to provide a standardized protocol for the internal linkage of equipment is the Ethernet local area network. The network was originally developed by Xerox Corp., and later adopted by Digital Equipment Corp. (DEC) and Intel Corp. IBM is expected to announce an open LAN support capability, and other vendors have introduced intelligent network control units that can enable dissimilar equipment and processors to transmit data.

With the increase of more flexible technology, the installed base of LAN connections is expected to grow to more than six million by 1992.[2] There are various LAN configurations that can be selected, depending on local needs (see Technical Note 5:3).

> Technical Note 5:3
>
> Configurations for local area networks include 1.) star configuration, which places processors at key positions in the network and feeds terminals into the network through these processors; 2.) a ring with nodes; and 3.) a tree system, or hierarchy. The optimal configuration for any particular environment will depend on the traffic patterns within the network, the number of workstations to be supported and requirements for accessing centralized rather than distributed processors, printers and storage devices.

Digital PBX

Another option for local communications is the digital private branch exchange (PBX). A PBX is a locally installed telephone system for internal communications, which connects with the public phone system for external communications needs. In a digital PBX, the voice signals are converted to digital format (just the opposite of the analog lines, which require a modem to convert digital computer signals to an audible form). The capability to transmit in digital format makes it possible to use a digital PBX for data communications, as well as voice.

Currently, there are some problems with attempting to use PBX systems for data transmission. Most do not have the transmission capacity of LANs. In addition, the various kinds of signals (voice, data) being carried on the same line end up competing for use of the line (a condition known as contention). The solution to this problem, for some vendors, is to offer multi-channel systems in which the voice and data signals are carried on separate channels, although controlled by the same central PBX.

Despite these problems, there is a trend toward integration of voice and data within the same system. A digital internal phone system may be designed to handle computer to computer transmission, facsimile transmission and video conferencing. Such an integrated network approach has high initial start-up costs because of the large-scale introduction of new equipment. However, this type of system can be adapted easily to new technology and applications, and provides a uniform way of dealing with total company communications requirements. Larger organizations may be able to achieve significant savings through economies of scale which will offset the initial investment. At present, the integrated digital PBX data communications network is difficult to justify for most small businesses.

SUMMARY

The primary difference between a CBMS and a local or distributed network is remote versus local control. Although there are many types of equipment that can be used to create a distributed network, all share a basic structure in which messages are sent directly from one point in the network, to another. Microprocessor technology supplies the intelligence needed to handle messaging functions at each individual node in a network.

Chapter 6 outlines the general capabilities that should be considered when evaluating EMS systems and services.

FOOTNOTES

1. K. Hafner, "Study Examines Future of OA Market," *Computerworld* 17 (36) (September 1983): 73.

2. John Seaman, "LANs Ready," *Computer Decisions* 15 (6) (June 1983): 134-151.

6

Evaluating Your Needs

This chapter provides an overview of the features that should be considered when selecting an EMS service. In a distributed network, these features are provided by the hardware selected. A CBMS may provide many of the same capabilities as part of the centralized service.

Prior to selecting a CBMS, a distributed approach or some combination of the two, an organization must carefully analyze its needs. Particular attention must be paid to the volume of message traffic and the question of whether a centralized or decentralized operation is needed.

TRAFFIC VOLUME

Each organization should carefully review its message traffic patterns to determine:

- How many messages are outgoing and how many are incoming;
- What the desired network access is, if other than DDD;
- What proportion of message traffic is intraorganizational, and what proportion is interorganizational;
- How many people need direct access to the message system.

The last item is an important consideration since, with very few exceptions, microprocessor-based products are designed for a single user. A large company, or one that has many people who wish to use the message system, will require a system that allows input from multiple terminals. This requirement limits the options to a very small number of hardware alternatives, and may be the deciding factor in selecting a CBMS over a distributed system.

CENTRALIZED VS. DECENTRALIZED INSTALLATIONS

There may be a tendency to serve communications needs throughout an organization by disbursing single-user systems to anyone who needs them. But in this situation each user will also need communications lines. In the case of TWX or telex service, the cost of numerous lines within one organization may be prohibitive. In the case of DDD access, the cost of the added lines may be smaller but will still be significant (and is likely to go higher as the effects of deregulation are felt).

For either network, having multiple communications lines and a decentralized communications operation will make it extremely difficult to maintain either budgetary or administrative control over the organization's communications costs, policies and procedures. It may also complicate user training and equipment and line maintenance. The seriousness of the technical and administrative problems introduced by decentralization will depend on the size, nature and objectives of each organization.

The most important areas to examine when evaluating any EMS product or service are:

- External networks and protocols;
- Concurrent operations;
- Composing and storing text;
- Transmission, connect and disconnect;
- Receiving messages;
- Traffic records;
- User interface;
- Integration with other operations.

Each of these points will be examined in further detail.

EXTERNAL NETWORKS AND PROTOCOLS

Communications requirements for an EMS will depend on the needs and applications of the individual user. A very basic decision that must be made at the outset is to determine which of the available communications networks need to be accessed. Each has different features, as shown in Table 6.1. Some companies may need only domestic DDD access. Others will need

Table 6.1: Features of External Communications Networks

Network	Scope	Characteristics
Telex	International	Dedicated line; 50-75 bps; point-to-point
TWX	International and domestic	Dedicated line; 110 bps; point-to-point
DDD	International and domestic	Switched line; 110-2400 bps; point-to-point; access to CBMS, interconnect services or IRC gateways
Leased line	International and domestic	Dedicated line, up to 50 Kbps; point-to-point

to communicate with the TWX or telex networks, either domestically or internationally. Many companies will have to access all of these plus others, such as private data networks or other systems. Each of the communications networks has its own data transmission specifications which your system must accommodate. The protocols on one may be unacceptable for another.

The value added networks (VANs) provide an alternate way of handling the need for multiple protocols. These networks are designed to accommodate devices with many different communications protocols, and can be very effective intermediaries between dissimilar and incompatible equipment. The electronic mail systems available from the VANs (e.g., Telemail, OnTyme) can be used to "translate" data from one system to another. This allows some functions (text creation, storage) to be handled locally on in-house equipment, while the VAN provides the protocol conversion functions.

Transmission Speed

One aspect of the network protocol that must be matched on each end is the transmission speed. This is normally represented in bits per second (bps). The most frequently used speeds on dial-up systems are 110 bps, 300 bps and 1200 bps. The use of conditioned or leased lines can allow speeds of up to many thousands of bits per second (Kbps). Use of these high speeds is almost never seen in systems devoted to message traffic alone, as the volume of traffic cannot begin to justify the expense.

Code

A second element that must be matched in the communications network is the code used. As noted in earlier chapters, the most common codes encountered in message systems are the ASCII code, which uses eight bits to represent 128 characters, and the Baudot code, which uses a five-bit pattern to represent 58 characters. The telex networks use Baudot; TWX and most of the other public networks use ASCII.

Transmission Mode

A third area of compatibility is the transmission mode, which can be either synchronous or asynchronous. Asynchronous transmission is far less efficient, but it is the dominant mode used in dial-up systems because its speed is adequate for the low volumes of data being handled, and the equipment is less costly.

There are other elements that make up the communications protocol as well: duplex transmission, answerback formats and handshaking procedures, meaning of control characters, etc. A mismatching of any of these elements will result in a failure to transmit, garbling of the transmitted data or worse.

Where dissimilar protocols are being used on each end of the link, at least one of the machines must be able to perform the needed conversions and adaptations in order for data to be exchanged successfully. This is accomplished either by adjusting the settings on the communications port, as instructed by the operator, or by providing a port for each network. The alternative is to have a separate machine for each system accessed, or to subscribe to an interconnect service that can provide the translations. (These services are described in Chapter 9.)

CONCURRENT OPERATION

In addition to selecting which networks are be accessed, the user must determine the number of ports or channels that are required in order to support concurrent operations. This consideration applies only to distributed processing. All commercial CBMS services support concurrent operations.

In a low traffic volume situation, only one or two ports may be required. In other circumstances, especially where traffic load is high or where several networks are being accessed, it may be essential to have four or more separate communications lines. An important point here, which may easily be overlooked, is that having multiple ports available does not guarantee that more than one can be in operation simultaneously. A microprocessor may not be able to handle multiple tasks at one time. Systems that do not provide fully concurrent operations may create bottlenecks which handicap the entire communications service.

It may be possible for incoming and outgoing calls to be received and sent simultaneously, even on the same network, depending on the number of available ports for that network and the ability to handle multiple tasks at one time. Even if this is not the case, it may be possible to continue with a local task, such as text preparation, while messages are being received. This is an important consideration, as otherwise, a busy communications station is going to be unable to receive any incoming calls during working hours—all transmissions will have to be completed at night, when messages are not being keyed.

COMPOSING AND STORING TEXT

How efficiently text can be composed and stored is an important equipment consideration for either a distributed processing or commercial CBMS service. The source of the text can be either direct entry online from the keyboard, offline from paper tape or from a temporary storage area (buffer) within the workstation itself (see Technical Note 6:1), or from another device, such as a word processor or personal computer. Figure 6.1 ranks these options in terms of their efficiency.

> Technical Note 6:1
>
> A buffer is a section of the RAM (random access memory) which is set aside for the temporary storage of data being transferred to or from the microprocessor. Text must be placed in or passed through the buffer before it can be transmitted over the communications line or saved in a disk file or other permanent storage.

Preparing Text for Transmission

Direct online keying is the least desirable, and microprocessor devices make it unnecessary. Even the paper tape used in older teletype machines is more accurate and efficient, and therefore less costly, than online keying. The tape can also be reused, to an extent, to repeat or duplicate a message. Most microprocessor-based electronic mail installations are designed either to prepare text internally with a text editing function, accept files from an external processor, or both.

The internal editor that is provided may be quite rudimentary, having limited space for messages and limited flexibility for formats. It can have only line-by-line editing, or be a full-screen word processing program with the ability to manipulate or duplicate blocks of text, make global changes, etc.

Figure 6.1: Efficiency of Text Composition and Storage Options

Least efficient ↓	Direct keyboard entry, online
	Paper tape entry, offline
	Workstation with local RAM and editor, offline
Most efficient	Word processor, disk files

Message Formatting

How messages are formatted by the EMS system is another important consideration. It is an evaluation criterion for both distributed processing equipment and CBMS services. Message formatting should be provided both for the "header" information (the answerback code, address, etc.) and for the body of the message (see Figure 6.2).

Automatic margins and page breaks may be available on the more advanced systems. Other systems may provide the user with fill-in-the blank forms, which are sometimes defined by the supplier and sometimes by the user. User-defined forms can greatly enhance productivity where standardized

Figure 6.2: Sample Electronic Mail Message

```
                    DIALCOM ELECTRONIC MAIL SERVICE


please log in: DIALCOM::63

Dialcom: call connected
Primecom Network 18.4G System 63

 Please Sign On
>ID IEM005 TRY
ITT Dialcom Computer Services 18.4G(63)
On At 2:51 06/20/84 EDT
Last On At 8:46 06/18/84 EDT

>MAIL

Send, Read or Scan:  READ

     To:  IEM005
   From:  IEM020    Posted:  Wed  20-June-84  3:08 EDT Sys 63  (6)
Subject:  VISIT

--More--

Are we still scheduled for a meeting next week regarding
our options for electronic mail service?
L. Trudell
```

Printed by permission of ITT Dialcom, Inc.

formats are required for submitting orders, requisitions, statistics and other such information.

Storing Prepared Text

Once the text is prepared, whether internally or externally, it must be stored until such time as it can be successfully transmitted. An EMS device must track the messages queued for channel and destination, and wait for the connection to be correctly established prior to transmitting. This is not a consideration with CBMS services, which handle this part of the operation.

Messages should be available for listing or review, and should be identified by date, destination or name. Further, it should be permissible to cancel or delay transmission of an outbound message without destroying the contents. A surprising number of systems do not allow message cancellation.

Transferring Files

Transferring files from an external editor to an EMS workstation has advantages, but users should be aware of compatibility restrictions—only limited types of equipment may be thoroughly compatible. Storage restrictions may still present a problem. Users should investigate how the equipment will handle files that are too large to be transferred, or uploaded, in a single operation (see Technical Note 6:2).

It is usually not necessary to worry about storage restrictions when transferring files to a CBMS. Uploading files from a local EMS workstation to a CBMS is a very efficient way of transferring large text files.

> Technical Note 6:2
>
> The term uploading is used to describe the process by which text or data stored in a local computer facility is transmitted to another remote computer facility. Generally, an entire file or block is transmitted at one time, which may require the use of a special command sequence to assure that the receiving computer is prepared to accept a long stream of transmitted data. The term downloading refers to the opposite process, in which a file is transferred from the remotely accessed computer and put into local storage. Systems designed for frequent uploading and downloading may provide special error-checking and file transfer monitoring capabilities, to assure that no data are lost or garbled during a transfer.

TRANSMISSION, CONNECT AND DISCONNECT

An important feature of any electronic mail system is the way in which connections are established between the sender and the recipient. In almost all cases this will be accomplished through some sort of dialing, but there are differences in the method and efficiency of this operation.

Making the Connection

Dialing may be accomplished manually (by the operator keying in the digits) or automatically. Manual dialing is a great disadvantage in an electronic mail system, as it requires that an operator be present each and every time a connection is attempted, whether or not the attempt succeeds. Automatic dialing allows the operator to key the desired number only once; from that point on the machine can redial it as many times as necessary. Most hardware designed for electronic mail can store more than one number; however, the storage capacity can vary widely and is also subject to limitations on the number of digits per number or the incorporation of pauses or other instructions.

Depending on which network is being accessed, and whether access is direct or through an intermediate network (for instance, Sprint or MCI), the number of digits may range from five to 20 or more. Since most hardware has preset limits on the number of digits that can be used to dial, this may become a problem. Again, depending on which network(s) is being used, it may be necessary for the dialed number to incorporate pauses as well as digits. This may also be prevented by hardware limitations; the necessary number of digits may exceed the capacity of the device doing the dialing.

The storage of numbers to be dialed should be linked to the communications network on which they are to be used, so that the selection of a number from memory automatically chooses and/or configures the communications port. Identification of the stored numbers by a name or code is usual, although not universal. This feature is usually described as providing a "directory." It is important to look at the format for the directory (i.e., is it easy to understand?) and the way in which it is accessed. If the directory must be checked by the operator during preparation of each message, it may not be even as useful as a Rolodex file. The system should be able to pull up directory information from the name or code alone.

Disconnecting from the System

Another useful function is automatic disconnection from the remote recipient once a transmission is completed. Most CBMS systems provide a "time-out" function—an automatic disconnection when no data have been transmitted or received for a predetermined length of time, usually one to 10 minutes. This prevents the user from becoming stuck online, and also prevents the tying up of a communications port simply because someone forgot to log-off.

Direct point-to-point message systems, whether TWX, telex or DDD, do not provide this function as part of the network. The line will stay open indefinitely unless a signal to disconnect is given by either the sender or the recipient. Because this creates the possibility of hours-long connections (and the associated charges) if such an incident should occur when no operator is present to disconnect manually, most of the microprocessor-based EMS systems will incorporate some provisions for an automatic termination, along with the unattended origination and acceptance of calls.

RECEIVING MESSAGES

In a CBMS, text is stored until the recipient is ready to receive the messages, so that receiving text is at the control of the user. However, in a distributed processing network, text is received at each local workstation when a message has been transmitted; thus, reception is not controlled by the user. Therefore, incoming message traffic in a distributed network should be handled with as little manual intervention as possible. The system must respond to the proper port, adjust to the appropriate network protocol (discussed above) and perform the appropriate handshaking with the transmitting device (see Technical Note 6:3).

Some EMS workstations will be unable to communicate except with identical devices; others will communicate with any equipment that can emulate their protocols.

> Technical Note 6:3
>
> Handshaking refers to the exchange of signals between two pieces of equipment. This exchange of signals establishes the connection between the two ends. It "verifies that the called and calling devices are the correct ones, establishes one device as the master (controller of the call) and one as the slave, ... determines the direction of the initial transmission and determines the mode in which the terminal is currently operating, such as idle or control mode. When in a control mode, the terminal is ready to accept or transmit a message."[1]

Storing Received Messages

It should not be necessary for an operator to be present in order for a message to be received. The incoming text may be displayed on a CRT, printed out or captured in a screen buffer and transferred to a printer later. Most of the newer systems provide some such storage, although it may be quite temporary or limited in capacity. This internal storage can be either electronic (RAM) or magnetic media (disk or tape).

Preference should be given to systems that both display or print the incoming messages, and also capture the text in storage. There are many instances when incoming text may need to become part of another message to be routed to another recipient. There are also compelling reasons for maintaining an archive of all message traffic, and this is much more conveniently and economically done with electronic media.

There is wide variation in the storage capacity available for such capturing of messages, depending on what medium is used. The space allocated for incoming calls may compete with that for text preparation or it may be entirely separate. Consideration should also be given to whether the capturing is automatic or if it is done only on operator command. Users should investigate what happens when the storage space is filled: Are incoming messages refused? Not captured? Do they overwrite previous messages? Is there any warning that this condition is about to occur?

Control Characters

Incoming text, whether it is being received from a CBMS or transmitted from another EMS workstation, may contain control characters or codes—instructions intended either for the device on which the text was prepared, for the communications network or for the receiving device (see Technical Note 6:4).

Unfortunately, the control characters' meanings are not totally standardized. When they were used only for data communications the meanings were clearer. Now that they are also being used for word processors and other microcomputer program operations, they can create tab stops, paragraph breaks, alternate character sets, reverse video or underscoring, or the deletion of words, characters, lines or, more disastrously, the erasing of entire messages or files. Thus, it is important to know how your system handles the transmission or receipt of these nonprinting characters.

> Technical Note 6:4
>
> Control characters are "a code generated by holding down the control key (often marked CTRL or CNTRL) while pressing another key, resulting in a different signal than the second key normally generates."[2] Usually associated with the 32 nonprinting ASCII codes, control characters are used to produce carriage returns, linefeeds, form feeds, backspaces and other such instructions. The meaning of a control sequence for any given device or program must be determined from that system's user documentation.

In some cases, given the difficulty of recognizing which ones are relevant, the equipment ignores all control codes. This is often the only safe option where dissimilar devices are being used by the sender and recipient. In other situations it may be possible to configure the device to respond only to designated codes and not others. Since the meaning of the codes is so often not standardized, and a misinterpretation can lead to disastrous results, an EMS device should be able to "strip out" unrecognized instructions. A useful feature to have is the ability to display, on demand, any control characters that are imbedded in messages or files. Even if the presence of control characters is suspected, it cannot be proved or prevented without this capability.

TRAFFIC RECORDS

Every good electronic mail system will need some method for recording the traffic on it. Outgoing messages should be tracked by network, recipient (number, name or both) and whether successfully transmitted or not. Additionally, it is useful if messages are flagged with such information as the date and time of transmittal, how many attempts were necessary (if more than one) and the length of the transmission either in time or other measure (characters, lines, etc.). If the system can estimate network charges, that is an obvious advantage. These records are needed primarily for billing purposes. Most users do not get involved in producing bills, but everyone has to pay them and it is a good idea to verify the accuracy of the charges before making payment.

Traffic records are also essential in designing, selecting or upgrading communications services. Existing loads and patterns must be known before decisions can be made as to what improvements are desired or needed. For this purpose, records must show more than just the gross number of messages. Message traffic must be broken down by network, destination or source, length, time of day, day of the week, time of the month or year, etc. All of this information is necessary in determining the optimum system configuration for the user—how many channels and user terminals are needed, which networks should be accessed, etc.

Traffic records will also facilitate better use of the existing system. They will identify bottlenecks or problem areas. They may show where the available transmission options are not being used in a cost-effective way. They will also show the workload and productivity of system users, and indicate where staff should be allocated or reassigned. All of these are important management considerations.

USER INTERFACE

In addition to performing all of the functions discussed above, an electronic mail system must be easy to use. If it is not, its use will be avoided by those it is most intended to benefit. There are some simple, common-sense features that can go a long way toward making an EMS acceptable to its users.

Equipment Features

Virtually every distributed EMS will have two operating modes, one for local interaction between the user and the system and another for interaction with the other remote users. If full concurrency of operation is provided, it may be possible to operate in both modes simultaneously; if not, there should be a clear indication of what the current status is, so that no accidental disconnections occur and no incoming messages are blocked unnecessarily.

For intelligent workstations, another useful and closely related feature is the provision of simple indicators that show what communications protocols are currently selected for each port. These can be lights, switches or a "status line" on the screen (usually at the top or bottom). If not continuously available, this information should at least be readily and simply displayed. Such provisions will help prevent or identify misfunctions such as unmatched protocols or overflowing memory.

Software or System Features

It is generally accepted that the best way to structure communications software is to make it menu-driven. This means that, for any function, the user is prompted to select from a menu of options. Certainly it is less of a strain on a person's memory to select from a list of choices than it is to remember what all the possible alternatives are. But the experienced user may become annoyed at having to look at a menu for every single operation, so these should either be kept to a minimum, or be able to be bypassed by a command structure. Since many messages follow a standard format, it is helpful if the system will prompt the user to fill in the form for each piece of information needed. This can be a predetermined format for the message header. Some systems allow users to define their own prompted forms for the internal message content.

User Manual

The user manual itself is a critical factor in the success of any EMS. Unfortunately, the failings may not reveal themselves until the user is tangled in error messages. Although good documentation does not guarantee a good system, poor documentation can ruin the usefulness of an excellent one.

INTEGRATING EMS WITH OTHER OPERATIONS

Inasmuch as possible, the EMS should be incorporated into the routine daily operations of the user. The varying types of EMS lend themselves to different degrees of integration. The LAN-based systems probably come the closest to total integration. CBMS services are at the other end of the spectrum, since these are external services which are accessed remotely. Therefore, CBMS services cannot be integrated with other office functions within the organization. Those office operations that are most likely to benefit from links to the message systems include the telephone system, internal or external data processing, and information retrieval functions.

Integration with the Telephone System

At present, it is difficult to achieve integration of the telephone system using microprocessor-based EMS workstations. A few workstations are being developed which do put both voice and text messages into one piece of hardware, but these are unusual (the DataVoice and the CoSystem workstations are examples).

Integration with Data Processing

Incorporation of internal or external data processing and data retrieval functions is much more readily accomplished. Virtually all of the microprocesser-based systems provide a way both to capture and manipulate incoming data; however, the limitations are on the amount and format of the data. For example, it may be easy to download and revise a brief text file, but one of any great size may be impossible to handle. Also, if the information to be downloaded contains special formats (as would be the case for most accounting or spreadsheet files) or graphics, it may not be possible to process. If sharing and reprocessing of data is desired, product choices will be limited to very few electronic mail systems.

SUMMARY

This chapter has examined the functions users should consider when evaluating any type of EMS equipment or service. As the discussion has shown, when an organization contracts with a CBMS for electronic mail service, the functions provided depend less on the type of equipment used to access the service, than on the service itself: many of the functions, such as concurrent operations and receiving messages, are provided by the CBMS.

However, when putting together a distributed or local EMS network, users must evaluate equipment and software carefully in light of the functions described. For this reason, Chapter 7 provides an in-depth examination of EMS equipment. Chapter 8 is devoted to the software packages available for microcomputers and communicating word processors.

FOOTNOTES

1. Jerry FitzGerald and Tom S. Eason, *Fundamentals of Data Communications* (New York: John Wiley & Sons, 1978).

2. Jeffrey Emmet Levinger and Robert Patrick Merges, *VISITERM User's Guide* (San Jose, CA: VisiCorp, Inc., 1982).

7

The Hardware Alternatives

The microprocessor-based hardware products used for electronic mail encompass a wide range of equipment. What sets them apart from the software-based electronic mail systems described in Chapter 8 is that all of the mail functions are "on board." That is, the programming that produces the electronic mail operations is in the actual circuitry of the hardware, or the firmware. These devices are not programmable by the user (although they offer a wide range of configurable settings) and cannot be used for any other functions except those of electronic messaging.

The two principle categories of hardware-based electronic mail products are stand-alone, dedicated message processing workstations and attachable intelligent peripherals. This chapter will evaluate each in terms of the functions identified in Chapter 6, and will describe the major workstations and peripherals available.

MESSAGE PROCESSING WORKSTATIONS

The most prevalent and sophisticated of the microprocessor-based EMS systems are the so-called message processing workstations or communications terminals. The terminology is vague for these devices, as no widely accepted definition exists. These products are in many cases the equivalent of a very powerful personal computer, but dedicated to the single purpose of handling communications and messaging functions. The hardware is custom-built, using proprietary design features, and includes the CRT display, one or more modems, memory (disk, tape or solid state) and usually an optional selection of printers.

Most manufacturers of these devices offer a wide range of models that can be configured to suit the customer's individual needs. (This is in contrast to both peripheral devices and microcomputer EMS software, which typically come in "one size only.") Of course, price is an influential factor, as the dedicated workstations range from two to 10 times the cost of other microprocessor-based products.

Communications terminals, being designed exclusively for messaging purposes, handle these functions extremely well. Storage is ample and forwarding is automatic, even to multiple destinations. Once the text is entered, virtually all operations can be conducted without operator involvement. Configurations can be matched to almost any desired protocols, so that message traffic can be exchanged with practically any communicating device. Security and privacy are carefully handled; in some cases data encryption is offered as well. In evaluating these dedicated workstations, it is clear that they are top-of-the-line microprocessor systems: there are few EMS functions at which they do not excel.

Compatibility with External Networks and Protocols

The original purpose of the dedicated workstations was to replace the old teletype terminals in the corporate mailroom. As communications networks have become more sophisticated, so have workstations. They can be supplied with protocols to match almost any communications need, for any public or private data network. All of the standard protocols are supported, and most non-standard ones can be configured by the user. High-speed, synchronous protocols allow direct communication with mainframes. Some products can support packet-switching protocols (X.25 and others)—even satellite connections may be supported.

Translations and links are provided that will transfer messages between any systems used. (This goes far beyond the simple TWX-to-DDD transfers, where the only difference in protocol is transmission speed.) All of the necessary handshaking is done automatically, without the operator having to be present.

Concurrent Operations

Of all the microprocessor-based EMS systems, the communications workstations are the only ones that provide completely concurrent operations. They can do this because they use microprocessors and operating systems that support a true multi-tasking environment. The dedicated workstations are also the most generous in the provision of communications ports and user stations. A number of these products can support as many as eight communications lines, and up to 16 user terminals, all operating simultaneously. Multiple messages can be composed at once, concurrently with the transmission and receipt of still other messages. While not many corporations will need such capacity, this does ensure that there will be little likelihood of messaging bottlenecks.

Composing and Storing Text

Since the stand-alone devices have such a wide range of compatibility, they can accept text prepared and transmitted by almost any device. (At least one can accept input from an optical character recognition, or OCR, device.) Excellent provision is made for internal message preparation. Text editors are provided by all of the products; several incorporate full-screen word processing and formatting. User-defined forms and screen prompts make message preparation fast and simple. The storage space available for messages may range up to 2 million characters, using either floppy or hard disk options. All stored files can be re-accessed for editing and retransmission.

Transmission, Connect and Disconnect

Most systems establish the connection to another message station by dialing automatically from a directory of names, numbers and answerbacks. The size of these directories is generous, with most allowing up to several hundred recipients to be stored. Distribution lists are supported, so that messages may be sent to multiple recipients automatically. The systems can batch transmissions to a single destination, so that multiple calls are not made to the same number. Messages can be flagged for particular individuals at a location; they can also be automatically forwarded from one location to another in sequence. All messages are automatically numbered for identification and given time and date headers.

Receiving Text

Communications terminals will acknowledge and accept incoming message traffic automatically. Most assign message numbers, time and date information to every incoming call, as well as storing the text. In multi-station installations, the text or a message alert may be routed to the proper station. The captured text can be translated for retransmission on another network, modified or printed as needed. With multiple communications lines and large amounts of storage, it is rare for incoming calls to be blocked by these systems.

The treatment of control characters is also seldom a problem, since so many protocols can be configured and matched automatically.

Traffic Records

It is in this area that the communications workstations can be most effective. The communications workstation acts in many ways as its own network controller, flagging and logging every transmission for date, time, network, duration, destination, etc. Many will estimate line charges as well. Compilations are possible, so that weekly or monthly records can be reviewed. Permanent storage on floppy disk can allow records analysis at any future time.

User Interface

The widespread acceptance of these workstations in organizations with a high volume of message traffic speaks well of their contributions to efficiency and cost reduction. Most of these systems take advantage of the customized hardware to offer clearly labeled function keys or switches that eliminate the need for extensive command structures. The use of menus is almost universal, so that screen prompts provide all the instruction needed for most functions.

Integration with Other Operations

Because the stand-alone communications terminals are designed for the heavily trafficked message center, there is little incentive to combine other functions onto a very specialized machine. To do so would only create unrealistic demands on an already heavily used piece of equipment.

The one area where some integration is occurring is the combination of data networks with voice messaging systems. Voice mail is gaining acceptance, although it is still not nearly as widespread as other forms of messaging. Workstations are beginning to be introduced (such as the DataVoice from Basic Telecommunications) which can capture voice messages onto tape as well as handle text messages. The digital PBX manufacturers will probably lead in this area, since these systems will have more resemblance to a central-processor local area network (LAN) than to the local intelligence microprocessor systems that are predominant now.

AVAILABLE MESSAGE PROCESSING WORKSTATIONS

Following are descriptions of the major message processing workstations available as of early 1984. Addresses and telephone numbers for the vendors whose products are listed below can be found in Appendix B. The features and characteristics of several message processing workstations are compared in Table 7.1.

American Teleprocessing Corp.*

The ATC 2500 multiport message handling system can accommodate four outgoing communications lines for TWX, telex, DDD and private networks or gateway services. It can also provide up to 15 user terminals for message input and delivery within the organization. High-volume traffic is accommodated by up to 2 megabytes of storage. Full text editing, multiple printers, 240-address directory and OCR input are provided.

Price: Contact vendor.

Basic Telecommunications Corp.*

The DataVoice is a desktop intelligent communications workstation that combines an advanced telephone, electronic calendar, voice mail and terminal functions. Automatic dialing and redialing of up to 60 stored numbers, automatic transmission/receipt of either text or voice messages, and simple function-key operation are featured. A 103 modem is standard, as is an RS-232 and a parallel port.

Price: $1295 to $1995

Carterfone Communications Corp.*

The Carterfone 7700 multiport communications terminal provides access to TWX, telex, DDD and IRC networks, with full concurrency on each line. Word processing and financial spreadsheet packages are available, in addition to the automatic message handling functions. A full range of service options is featured.

Price: $2795 to $3495

C & W Incotel, Ltd.

The Incotel MX 100 is a store-and-forward message and data switching system, based on a PDP-11/23 CPU. The 128K RAM is supplemented by both a floppy disk and a 20 megabyte hard disk, for storage of several hundred messages. Automatic dialing and formatting are provided for TWX, telex and DDD, as well as private networks. System traffic reports

---

*Product appears in comparison chart given in Table 7.1.

Table 7.1: Comparison of Message Processing Workstations

Feature	ATC 2500	Basic Data-Voice	Carter-fone 7700	Extel Com–Master	Henricksen Comm Center III	Sideral Micronet
Messaging						
Header with time/date	X		X	X	X	X
with sender/recipient			X	X	X	X
with subject heading				X		
Multiple recipients	X	X	X	X	X	
Message forwarding	X		X	X		
Message cancelling	X		X		X	
Message acknowledgment			X	X	X	
List incoming mail	X			X	X	
List outgoing mail	X			X	X	
Save received or sent mail	X	X	X	X	X	
File Storage						
Private files	X	X	X	X	X	
Shared (designated access)				X		
Public (unrestricted access)						
Message/File Retrieval						
By date	X	X				
By sender/recipient						
By subject						
By system assigned number	X	X	X		X	
Bulletin Board				X	X	
Conferencing						
Online chatting (two users)	X	X	X	X	X	X
Conference (three or more users)		X			X	
Text Manipulation						
Line editor	X	X	X	X		X
Formatting (paging, etc.)	X		X	X		
Full screen editor	X	X	X	X	X	X

Table 7.1: (cont.)

Feature	**ATC 2500**	**Basic Data-Voice**	**Carter-fone 7700**	**Extel Com-Master**	**Henricksen Comm Center III**	**Sideral Micronet**
User Aids						
Menus/command prompting	X	X	X	X	X	
Online help instructions		X				X
User defined forms		X	X	X	X	
Delivery Options						
Outdial to user terminal	X	X	X		X	X
Direct telex/TWX	X	X	X	X	X	X
First class mail						X
Mailgram	X			X	X	X
Interconnect to other EMS	X	X		X	X	X
Communications Networks						
Public telephone (dial-up DDD)	X	X	X	X	X	X
Private telephone (leased line)	X	X		X	X	X
Telex, TWX	X	X	X	X	X	X
LAN, coaxial cable		X				
LAN, twisted pair cable	X	X		X		
Transmission Speeds						
50 bps				X		X
110 bps	X		X	X	X	X
300 bps	X	X	X	X	X	X
1200 bps	X	X	X	X	X	X
2400 bps or higher				X		
Ports Available						
Communications lines (maximum)	8	1	4	4	2	4
User I/O stations (maximum)	16	1	1	1	1	1

can be obtained hourly, daily or on demand. Group address lists and multiple addressing are supported.

Price: Contact vendor.

Extel Corp.*

The Extel ComMaster is a message terminal that allows up to four communications ports, configured for any of eight interfaces, Varying storage media are available (RAM, floppy diskette or hard disk), and two local serial ports are provided for printers or other devices. Messages can be prepared, edited and reviewed concurrently with transmission/receipt of other messages. All message addressing and formatting is done automatically to match network requirements.

Price: $3800

Henriksen Data Systems, Inc.*

The Comm Center III has two communications ports and up to 32K of storage. Full screen editing is offered. All messages are automatically numbered and time/date stamped. All operations are fully concurrent, for simultaneous message preparation, transmission and receipt.

Price: $4995

International Digital Electronics Associates

The BITELEX is a multi-language communications station capable of operating on the TWX, telex or DDD networks. Its two communications ports can be configured to numerous protocols. Any character set can be accommodated, making it of special interest for international use. The unit has dual disk drives and can run any CP/M program. A dot matrix impact printer is built into the CRT chassis. Fully concurrent multi-tasking operations are supported.

Price: $3500

Lane Telecommunications

The Lane Silent Partner series provides automatic communication of TWX, telex and DDD messages. A CRT terminal, printer, disk storage and controller unit are included, with a back-up power supply for memory retention during power outages. A second CRT can be installed for simultaneous message preparation by two users. A directory stores numbers, answerbacks and formats for frequently used addresses. All transmission and receipt of messages is automatic. Network activity is recorded, showing status of any or all calls. Incoming calls are automatically filed for one or more recipients.

Price: $4600 to $10,500

Mohawk Data Sciences (MDS)

MDS uses its WINC Messenger terminals for access to its own worldwide communications network. The polled system automatically checks each station at regular intervals for message pick-up and delivery. Connections to domestic and international carriers are provided, with automatic protocol conversion. All messsages are confidential and secured from all but the sender and recipient.

Price: $5995

OKI Electric Industry Co., Ltd.

The OKI MT 100 N is an intelligent teleprinter with CRT display and floppy disk memory. Designed to facilitate use of the international communications network, it has 30K RAM for internal message editing and storage. A paper tape option is also available. The printer can handle either Latin or Arabic alphabets. A directory of 20 telex numbers can be stored, with a seven-day battery back-up.

Price: Contact vendor.

Sidereal Corp.*

The Micronet series of multiport communications terminals can provide from one to eight communications lines and can support from one to three local CRTs. Each model is fully upgradable, and capabilities can be added as needs dictate. An optional "archival" RAM allows 65K storage for incoming messages or messages to be held and sent later. Editing and local diagnostics are standard. Protocol conversion is automatic, so that messages can be exchanged among any of the networks.

Price: $3600 to $6300

3M Business Communications Products Div.

Among the many communications products offered by 3M is the Whisper

Exchange. It provides a centralized store-and-forward EMS system using up to eight ports for either dial-up or leased DDD lines. The BBN Infomail software is used. A 16-megabyte hard disk provides message storage.

The 3M "Whisper Switch" provides access to the international telex and TWX networks, as well as private and public DDD lines. Automatic code conversion and speed detection is supported. The message buffer can be expanded from 128K to 512K. Detailed billing and chargeback data are kept for all messages, with continuously accumulated traffic statistics.

Price: Contact vendor.

INTELLIGENT PERIPHERAL DEVICES

Peripheral systems refer to hardware devices that are designed to enhance the user's standard terminal, word processor or personal computer. The peripheral incorporates the modem itself, the programming or software necessary to control both the modem and the EMS functions, and the memory area where messages and directories are stored.

Peripheral devices fill an intermediate position in the spectrum of microprocessor-based EMS systems. They have greater flexibility and more features than microcomputer software products, but less than the stand-alone communications processors. They also fall between the other categories in terms of cost and market penetration. The peripherals are attractive because they allow the customer to upgrade from a dumb terminal or teletype without incurring the expense of a stand-alone message system, and without the line contention and other complex problems of a microcomputer software package.

Peripheral devices are generally delivered as replacements for existing dumb modems. Some are designed to be installed inside specific brands of terminals or personal computers. But whether delivered as a separate "box" or as an internal circuit board, they will encompass both the modem and the EMS functions.

When evaluated against the checklist of EMS functions, peripherals score well on nearly every criteria. All of these devices have internal storage for store-and-forward operations; all of them can operate unattended. In fact, many of them can operate independently of the terminal or microcomputer to which they are connected, performing mail functions "in the background" while other operations are running. Most can provide simultaneous preparation and transmission of messages. Compatibility is only occasionally a problem, since they attach to the local terminal through a standard RS-232 interface and can be configured to match many communications protocols.

Security and privacy are the weakest points for the peripherals. Often, any on-site user has access to all EMS files and functions. This aspect of peripheral design should be viewed in the context of the small office for which they are intended; security is less of a concern when the number of staff is very small.

Compatibility with External Networks and Protocols

The peripheral systems are available with ports for both the TWX/telex network and low-speed (up to 1200 bps) DDD access. This is done by providing separate communications lines for each network. Very rarely can more than two lines be supported. Those peripherals that support both the DDD and TWX/telex networks will usually reconfigure their protocols automatically for whichever is being accessed. Some peripherals will support the necessary mainframe speeds and protocols for private data network access, but since this is not their primary intended use, such capability is not common.

Concurrent Operations

Virtually all intelligent peripherals are designed to be single-user systems, supporting input/output from only a single workstation. A fair number of them do support internal multiple tasking, so that message transmission and receipt does not interfere with message composition. The concurrent operation may not extend to transmitting on one line while accepting a call on another, however. Most of the units that have multiple communication ports will allow only one to be active at a time.

One type of concurrency which the peripherals can offer is the ability to operate independently of the machine to which they are attached. This means that the local workstation, be it a terminal, word processor or microcomputer, can be switched to another completely separate operation (or turned off), while the peripheral continues to transmit and receive messages with its own on-board memory and software. This feature is a significant advantage, since it allows a single piece of equipment to be used for other functions, while retaining 24-hour-a-day EMS operations. This is in marked contrast to the microcomputer software EMS systems, which are dedicated to a single task when the mail system is running.

Composing and Storing Text

Peripherals offer a wide range of options for message creation. All of them allow for direct online keying, should that be needed for access to interactive systems. All of them also allow for keying text into internal memory for later transmission. In the majority of products, a simple text editor is provided for modifying and correcting the text prior to transmission. In some, text can also be loaded from a personal computer or word processor file, although the text may then be stripped of its formatting characters when it is transmitted.

A few peripherals may go beyond providing a simple line editor to allow movements of blocks of text or creation of user-defined forms. These features are quite useful, as they allow text to be automatically supplied with standard message headers or formats for the various networks or destinations. Some products offer user-defined forms and prompting.

The amount of storage space available in the peripherals varies widely, ranging from less than 10,000 characters to more than 100,000 characters. Some include a disk option for further memory expansion. Memory can be allocated on a permanent or case-by-case basis for outgoing messages, incoming messages, directory listings, etc.

Transmission, Connect and Disconnect

As noted above, the peripherals rate well in their capability for unattended operation. All will store directories of telephone numbers and dial the number when directed by the clock/calendar. The directories may hold as few as eight or as many as 700 entries. Most are intended to identify destination sites, rather than a mailbox or recipient at that site. Many incorporate network and answerback information in the directory, so that the correct protocols, communications line and handshaking will be selected automatically when the message is queued for sending.

The directories are compiled manually from the keyboard; there is no automatic updating as new destinations are dialed. Both rotary and tone dialing are available. Automatic log-on protocols for the various networks can be stored and used for both attended and unattended sign-on, and this information can be protected by a password.

Receiving Text

All of the peripherals will accept incoming calls automatically, either storing the text in memory or routing it to a printer. Most register a busy signal when the memory is full. Some peripherals have an indicator light that flashes when stored messages have not yet been read. Since the memory capacity is limited, not all will allow incoming text to be saved within the device for reuse.

The handling of control characters in incoming messages varies with the protocol being used. Those that support private data network protocols will generally not alter the control sequences; in other cases, the codes may be stripped out. Most commonly, the peripherals are limited to ASCII text files.

Traffic Records

Provision of traffic records is minimal with these systems. At best they can give a current status display of the contents of the memory, listing any queued messages awaiting transmission or printing. Because of memory limitations, comprehensive records are not maintained.

However, even these brief listings provide more information than is available to the user of the dumb terminal or teletype, which the peripherals are designed to enhance. It allows automatic daily tracking of the number of messages sent and received, and from whom; in some cases, the record will also show the duration of the call. This is considerably more convenient than tracking such data manually, and does allow some degree of checking to be done against service bills.

User Interface

Some of the peripherals have excellent design features that allow them to be used with almost no training. Screen prompting, indicator lights and simple mnemonic command structures make the devices simpler to use and understand than direct interaction with some networks.

Not all of the peripherals give as much consideration to this area, however, and this should be weighed carefully in terms of the number and level of expertise of the staff who will need to be trained. Of course, those peripherals which rely on an external word processor or editor to compose text will be easier to learn to use in themselves than those with internal editors. In these cases, one should evaluate how well the two command structures are integrated, and how difficult the transfer of data is between them.

Integration with Other Operations

The peripherals are not designed to integrate multiple office functions, although they are intended to enhance an important piece of equipment, allowing it to perform operations that may have previously required several different terminals. Data retrieval may also be enhanced if the device can be used to download information from the interactive systems. Each of these functions themselves, however, remain separate—only the hardware becomes integrated.

At least one peripheral, the Cygnet CoSystem, does attempt to integrate function as well as hardware. The CoSystem adds voice telephone capability to the IBM PC—its fully concurrent operation allows data on the screen to be transmitted and discussed via a simultaneous voice connection. Devices of this type will probably become much more common in the future, as penetration of the personal computer into the business setting increases. Manufacturers of intelligent terminals are also introducing voice telephone options on their machines. These have fewer capabilities than a microcomputer, but are available for about one fourth the cost.

AVAILABLE INTELLIGENT PERIPHERALS

As of early 1984, a few intelligent peripherals were on the market. Addresses and telephone numbers for the manufacturers of the six products described below are provided in Appendix B. The features and characteristics of several intelligent peripherals are compared in Table 7.2.

BetaCom*

The BetaCom PCM (Professional Communications Manager) works with a standard CRT terminal or personal computer. A basic text editor for message composition is provided, with 64K RAM (upgradable to 128K). A wide variety of protocols can be supported, including TWX, telex, standard ASCII, IBM 3270 and 3780, Hewlett-Packard 1000/3000 and Data General DG Nova/Eclipse. Delayed transmissions are controlled by the clock/calendar. Self-diagnostics are included, and the unit comes with either selectable pulse or tone dialing.

Price: $1800

Product appears in comparison chart given in Table 7.2.

Table 7.2: Comparison of Intelligent Peripherals

Feature	BetaCom PCM	Cygnet CoSystem	Microcom PCS/2000	Visionary 100
Messaging				
Header with time/date	X	X	X	
with sender/recipient	X	X	X	
with subject heading	X	X	X	
Multiple recipients	X	X		
Message forwarding		X		
Message cancelling	X	X		
Message acknowledgment		X	X	
List incoming mail	X	X	X	
List outgoing mail	X	X	X	
Save received or sent mail	X	X	X	
File Storage				
Private files	X	X	X	
Shared (designated access)	X			
Public (unrestricted access)				X
Message/File Retrieval				
By date		X		
By sender/recipient	X	X		
By subject		X		X
By system assigned number			X	
Bulletin Board				
Conferencing				
Online chatting (two users)		X	X	X
Conference (three or more users)		X		
Text Manipulation				
Line editor	X	X		
Formatting (paging, etc.)				
Full screen editor				

(Table 7.2 continued on next page)

Table 7.2: (cont.)

Feature	BetaCom PCM	Cygnet CoSystem	Microcom PCS/2000	Visionary 100
User Aids				
Menus/command prompting	X	X	X	
Online help instructions	X	X		X
User defined forms	X			
Delivery Options				
Outdial to user terminal	X	X	X	X
Direct telex/TWX	X	X		X
First class mail				
Mailgram				
Interconnect to other EMS	X	X	X	X
Communications Networks				
Public telephone (dial-up DDD)	X	X	X	X
Private telephone (leased line)	X			X
Telex, TWX	X			X
LAN, coaxial cable				
LAN, twisted pair cable	X			
Transmission speeds				
50 bps				
110 bps		X	X	
300 bps	X	X	X	X
1200 bps	X	X	X	X
2400 bps or higher				
Ports Available				
Communications lines (maximum)	1	3	1	1
User I/O stations (maximum	1	1	1	1

Chat Communications

The Chat II intelligent modem attaches to a terminal, word processor or personal computer to provide access to the TWX, telex and DDD networks on a single communications port. A directory lists up to eight frequently-called numbers; all protocol conversion is automatic, as is time and date tracking. The standard 16K memory is upgradable in 16K increments; floppy diskettes are optional. A front panel digital clock and full battery back-up are included.

Price: $1645

Cygnet Technologies, Inc.*

The communications CoSystem incorporates telephone and mail functions into the IBM pc. The attachable handset and keypad have 90K memory, programmable for single-key access to any host or number. A 400-name directory can be searched by name or department. Messages can be routed to stored distribution lists, or sent with other files (spreadsheets, etc.). A calendar function tracks appointments as well as message traffic. Simultaneous voice and data conversations are featured.

Price: $1495 to $1995

Microcom, Inc.*

The Professional Communication System (PCS/1200/300) is a modem designed for both terminals and personal computers. It performs unattended message transmission and receipt over a single DDD line. For message storage, 48K of memory is available. A separate printer port is provided, with speed buffering. Both text and binary files can be transmitted. Battery back-up is provided.

Price: $595 to $1095

Teleface Corp.

The TelexPlug connects to word processors or personal computers via an RS-232 port, which may be shared with another device, such as a printer. It provides 8K (optional 28K) storage for messages. Answerback verification and redialing for busy numbers are supported. Incoming messages can be captured automatically, from either TWX or telex.

Price: $1485

Visionary Electronics*

The Visionary 100 intelligent modem can be used with any terminal or personal computer via an RS-232 port. It provides 48K storage for a telephone directory, message preparation/receipt or other user files. Automatic, unattended transmission and receipt of messages includes date and time recording. A single communications line supports DDD at 300 or 1200 bps.

Price: $795 to $1095

SUMMARY

Intelligent peripheral attachments for terminals, word processors and personal computers offer significant advantages over dumb modems or one-network, one-machine installations. They can replace or enhance existing equipment at very minimal cost, and require no specialized installation or service agreements. The internal clock/calendar and message queuing can save transmission costs and increase operator efficiency. The automatic network selection and directory features reduce errors and training problems. Storage, while limited, is adequate for most low-volume users. Unattended operation is perhaps the greatest advantage of intelligent peripherals over the non-intelligent systems which they are designed to replace.

Where the message traffic requires multiple input stations and more than one or two communications lines, a dedicated workstation is the better choice. The completely concurrent operations and the ability to support almost any network or protocol requirements make these systems unmatched by any other microprocessor-based EMS product. The high initial cost of the equipment can be quickly recovered in more efficient operations. The extensive traffic reporting records are an important feature for a high-volume site, and, in addition, can provide documentation of the reduced operating costs.

In Chapter 8, we will examine the EMS software packages that can be used to turn microcomputers into EMS workstations. In addition, we will evaluate a hybrid product—communicating word processors.

8

The Software Alternatives

This chapter examines the software alternatives for EMS. Chiefly, these are the communications packages designed to run on microcomputers. In many ways it is difficult to separate software from the hardware which supports and runs it, since very little software is truly transportable from machine to machine without considerable modification. Most of the software packages to be described here will operate on only a specific brand of microcomputer. However, what sets these products apart is that they exist and are delivered as software. The progamming is not on-board in the firmware of the machine, as is true with the hardware-based products; therefore, the machine can be used for other functions when not dedicated to electronic mail.

There are also hybrid systems that contain elements of both the hardware-based and the software-based products. These often require a hardware modification or addition to enable them to run the appropriate software to create an electronic mail operation. Included in this hybrid category are communicating word processors and personal computers used in a cluster or local area network (LAN) configuration. However, in many ways these hybrids have characteristics very similar to the "strictly software" products, and therefore will be considered here.

CHARACTERISTICS OF EMS SOFTWARE NETWORKS

The EMS packages which support individual microcomputers communicating over DDD lines are few in number, and more limited in capability than many of the single-function, microprocessor-based products. However, some products do exist that will allow a group of remote micros to operate as an electronic mail network. Examples of such products are Micro-Courier for the Apple and Transend for Apple and IBM machines.

EMS software packages run on noncustomized hardware that is strictly off-the-shelf. This is one of their most appealing characteristics, since it means that the start-up costs can be held down through competitive bidding, and local service will be readily available. The only caveat is that for true electronic mail service, all installations in the network must have identical configurations. Communication between nonidentical hardware and software is possible only in a "dumb terminal" mode. This means that each site in the network must have the same microcomputer, modem and software in order to fully participate and take advantage of all of the mail functions.

Of the six basic EMS functions identified in Chapter 6, microcomputer software can do a good job on only three or four. Store-and-forward capability is provided through disk storage and the clock/calendar control of the modem. Unattended reception of messages is supported, although only when the system is "ready"—if another software package is being operated, incoming messages will be blocked. Simultaneous message preparation and transmission is rarely found on micros, because their operating systems cannot support more than one task at a time. Thus, each function must be done in sequence.

Lack of wide compatibility is the most obvious failing of the microcomputer EMS programs. They are compatible only with their own clones; none of the mail functions are supported with other microcomputer models or other mail packages. As stated previously, the only communication with nonmatching devices is in a dumb terminal emulation mode. Security and privacy are only moderately provided, through the use of IDs and passwords.

TYPES OF MICROCOMPUTER EMS SOFTWARE

The software packages sold for EMS have a very wide range of capabilities, and this can be a real problem for the user who is trying to select one. A major source of confusion is the tendency of software producers to claim "electronic mail" capability for every communications package, whether or not this is strictly true. Communications software runs the gamut from very elementary terminal emulation programs—which do practically nothing except to allow the microcomputer to access dial-up services (among which may be electronic mail)—to full-function message switching or store-and-forward mailbox systems.

The following are the range of capabilities provided by commercial communications packages, beginning with the most basic.

- Dumb terminal emulation
- Smart terminal emulation

- Bulletin board host
- TWX/telex emulation
- Electronic mail network

This chapter will be primarily concerned with TWX/telex emulation software and software that provides a full range of EMS services. First, we will briefly discuss the more basic types of packages to clarify their relationship to EMS.

DUMB AND SMART TERMINAL EMULATION PROGRAMS

These are communications and file transfer programs that allow microcomputers and word processors to communicate over the phone lines, with mainframes or with each other. The software packages allow micros to send and receive ASCII files using asynchronous protocols. As noted above, they "provide" electronic mail only in the sense that they enable users to access services that provide it. There are probably close to 150 of these packages on the market, although the current trend is to incorporate such software into the modem or the serial interface board (see Technical Note 8:1).

The primary distinction between dumb and smart terminal emulation programs is that smart programs usually provide some storage capacity or memory, to store telephone numbers or log-on sequences.

> Technical Note 8:1
>
> Many micrompeters do not come equipped with a port for generating serial signals. For them to do so, it is necessary to install a "serial interface," an additional circuit board that is inserted into one of the available slots or positions in the micro. Even fewer come equipped with a modem. This needs to be purchased separately, along with the software to run it.

ELECTRONIC BULLETIN BOARDS

A number of electronic bulletin board (EBB) software packages claim to offer electronic mail. This may not be quite true. They do allow a single microcomputer with a modem to act as a "host" that other microcomputers can dial into, to scan any notices that have been posted by other users. However, this is not done in real time. There are rarely any private mail boxes, no traffic records showing delivery/receipt for each message, no capacity for storing and reusing text and usually no directory of participants, although some do issue passwords for access. Most boards are completely public and open to anyone who knows the telephone number. The majority are designed by and for computer clubs, not business communications, and will not be considered further here.

TWX/TELEX EMULATION SOFTWARE

A more specialized kind of terminal emulation software is the package that allows the microcomputer to imitate the telex protocol, so that the micro can be connected directly to the telex network. These packages, too, are not really providing electronic mail services, although they are a considerable upgrade from the dumb teletype terminal.

This type of software package has been recommended as a way of reducing telex costs. "In general, the computer costs are lower because a telex or similar machine need not be leased....Computers are more accurate than telex machines (they check each character), are more responsive (a computer will only transmit if it has received a signal, called a handshake, from the receiving computer) and are frequently faster and permit checking and editing of data before [they are] transmitted. All in all...computers frequently incur lower charges, not because the rates are lower, but because they are more efficient to operate."[1]

TWX/TELEX EMULATION SOFTWARE PACKAGES

Given the widespread use of the TWX/telex network, this type of software package is attractive, especially to businesses with a substantial amount of telex traffic. Some examples of TWX/telex emulation software packages are described below. (Addresses and telephone numbers for the vendors listed can be found in Appendix B.) All prices given are as of 1984 and should be used for comparison only. Readers are urged to contact the manufacturer directly for the most current information.

Specific program features and characteristics are compared in Table 8.1, on page 117.

Advanced Micro Techniques

Two software packages are offered that allow CP/M-based microcomputers with standard modems to have easy, automatic access to the TWX/telex networks and to Western Union's Easylink store-and-forward message service. MicroTLX actually connects to the TWX network; telex access is via the Infomaster computer service. MicroTLX supports automatic dial/redial, but not unattended transmission. Incoming calls may be unattended; they will interrrupt any other operation. MicroEZlink simplifies access to the Easylink service by automatically formatting each message, including the sign-on protocol and the address. It supports a directory of frequently used addresses, and has an integral word processor. Menus and help screens are provided.

Price: $150

CAPPCOMM Software, Inc.*

Postman is an expandable menu-driven software package that allows the IBM PC to send and receive messages through the EasyLink service. Formats are automatically added to messages prepared using any word processing software package. Messages can have multiple recipients. Unattended message receipt is supported.

Price: $349

Cawthon Scientific Group

Two software packages connect CP/M-based microcomputers with modems to the TWX network and to the Easylink service. TXL: Telex Link allows the microcomputer to replace a telex machine by automatically formatting and transmitting messages composed on micro. Incoming messages are logged with date and time. CTL: Computer Telex Link is designed specifically for use with the Easylink service. It automatically performs the sign-on, formatting and addressing required for each message.

Price: $195 to $395

---

*Product appears in the comparison chart given in Table 8.1.

Microcom, Inc.

Micro/Telegram is a software package for Apple II microcomputers that formats messages for the Western Union network. A directory of up to 100 addresses and 26 distribution lists can be maintained. Unattended operation with automatic dial/redial can be scheduled with the clock/calendar. The software is designed for use with the Hayes Micromodem and an installed TWX line. Numerous menus control all operations.

Price: NA

SGS Semicondutor Corp.

Telex Plus is a group of software packages that allow microcomputers to functionally replace telex machines. The software runs under the SUNIX operating system, and provides automatic logging of messages, easy formatting for telex or Infomaster service, and simple editing capabilities. From one to seven users, and up to seven telex lines can be supported.

Price: $495 for telex $795 for TWX

Softest, Inc.*

SofGram is a software package for UNIX and UNIX look-alike systems that will improve the user interface with the TWX, telex and DDD networks by providing simple menus and preformatted screens. SofGram can run as a multi-user system, and can be configured for any ASCII terminal. A screen editor is provided, along with dial/redial, answerback validation, error handling and handshaking features. The program works either via a direct connection to the TWX/telex networks or through a gateway service. Mailing lists and message logging are supported. The software can run "in the background" while other computer functions are operating.

Price: $750

ELECTRONIC MAIL SOFTWARE

These are packages that are designed to be used on existing microcomputer equipment to provide true electronic mail as defined in this book. An in-house electronic mail network set up using this type of software has the advantage of using equipment that is already in place and that can be used for other functions. However, since usually only one communications line is provided, each user can only be connected to one other user at a time. Thus, this type of network is suitable only for businesses that have a very low volume of message traffic. (Expansion of this type of network is possible with the introduction of a local area network, described in Chapter 5.)

Because of this limitation, EMS software packages are unable to match the capabilities and scope of service offered by a commercial CBMS or an in-house network using equipment dedicated to EMS (such as message processing workstations). This may be one reason why so few true EMS software packages are available for microcomputers. When EMS software is evaluated against the checklist of functions given in Chapter 6, limitations are found in nearly every category.

External Networks and Protocols

The available microcomputer EMS programs support only a single communications protocol (serial, aynchronous, ASCII) when operating as a mail system. Other protocols (for TWX/telex or private data networks) are supported only in a dumb terminal mode, and may be limited to providing direct connections to a mainframe. The microcomputer EMS is limited to a single communications network—the DDD. Files and messages prepared under the EMS software are not compatible with other protocols, and, therefore, cannot be sent on the TWX/telex network or private data networks. The transmisson speed within the EMS program is limited to low speeds (1200 bps maximum).

Concurrent Operation

Microcomputer operating systems have only very recently been able to support multiple tasking. Until the EMS software packages can be rewritten for the newer operating systems, they will not be able to have messages transmitted or received while text is being composed or read, and vice versa. They also cannot perform any electronic mail functions while another software package is running. Another aspect is the single-user nature of the microcomputer. As a workstation, it can only support one user at a time. If many people at a location wish to prepare and send messages, line contention problems may arise.

Since these limitations are imposed by the microcomputer operating system, one cannot blame the designers of the existing EMS software products.

However, the restrictions—especially when coupled with the limitation of a single communications line—make the systems suitable for low volume applications only, as mentioned above. As multi-user operating systems become more widely supported on microcomputers, new software should also become available which will resolve these problems.

Composing and Storing Text

Microcomputers offer a considerable advantage for composing and storing text, since the storage space for messages is limited only by the amount of floppy or hard disk space available. Messages can generally be composed using both the EMS program and a compatible word processor program, giving the user flexibility in text formatting and manipulation. The disk-stored text is relatively "safe" storage, being much less susceptible to accidental erasure than the RAM storage used in many of the peripheral and stand-alone EMS products.

Typically, messages composed using the EMS program's internal text editor will be limited in length to only a few thousand characters. Longer reports or documents must be prepared externally using a compatible word processor program, and loaded as a disk file. The internal editor may lack some of the conveniences of a word processor—such as rearranging blocks of text, making global changes or formatting text—another reason for using external software.

It is important to note, though, that when messages or files are prepared using an external program, they may be transmitted in an "untranslated" format. This means that they can only be read or edited at the receiving end by using the same external program. This is not a problem with a microcomputer or word processor network, as they are made up of identical installations and the same programs are apt to be available at all locations. However, if there is a need to transfer files from the EMS program to other mail networks or systems, this incompatibility may stand firmly in the way.

Transmission, Connect and Disconnect

All microcomputer EMS programs are designed for use with modems that can support automatic dialing and redialing of stored numbers. The electronic telephone directories contained in the programs will usually accommodate very long numbers, to allow for access codes, pauses for dial tones, etc.

All microcomputer EMS software has an internal clock/calendar, which supplies a time and date header for each message. This allows messages to be set for transmission at any desired hour or day. When unattended, the computer may be set for transmit only, receive only, or both send and receive. Blocked calls are redialed as many as 10 times at set time intervals.

Messages can be sent to individual mailbox IDs or routed over distribution lists. The number of mailboxes that can be supported by microcomputer EMS software ranges from one hundred to several hundred; up to a few dozen distribution lists can be supported. The number of messages that can be queued for transmission is often limited to the capacity of one disk. Automatic disconnection is generally provided, so that the communications line is used efficiently, but this should be examined if unattended operation is to be used extensively. On some systems it is possible to dial up another location and retrieve messages or files that are stored there. Where this feature is present, password protection is needed to control access.

Receiving Messages

The receiving end must have a direct incoming DDD line (i.e., not through a switchboard) in order to accept messages. Handshaking protocols are preset by the software. As stated, in most cases only calls from an identical installation can be accepted. The software cannot alter its handshaking protocol to take calls when unattended from other EMS programs or to function in a dumb terminal mode.

Upon receipt, messages are usually captured onto a disk; when the disk is full no additional calls are accepted. In networks where one site has heavier traffic than the others, it may be advisable to use a hard disk to provide sufficient capacity. In most systems, the incoming messages are flagged for the intended recipient, so that it may be possible to have multiple mailboxes at one telephone number. The received messages can be printed, deleted or saved for future use.

Traffic Records

The traffic records kept by microcomputer EMS systems are necessarily limited by the fact that these networks are operated in a point-to-point style. Each installation will have records of its own incoming and outgoing messages, but no installation will have records for the network as a whole. This is not a criticism; it is a characteristic of any noncentralized EMS system. The traffic log function may be a part of the mail scanning operation of the software, which lists waiting messages or newly received messages, typically with the header information. Traffic records may be limited to a single session of transmitting and receiving; if there is no capability to compile (probably daily) these brief records into a more comprehensive record, this may be a drawback.

User Interface

Microcomputer EMS systems rate well in this respect, since they make good use of menu structures. There is rarely any necessity for extensive training on the EMS operation, although training may be needed for the micro itself. The user does have to be familiar enough with the microcomputer to be able to deal with its operating system and its peripherals, and to be able to differentiate between other operations and those of the EMS software. Other software, such as a word processing package being used to prepare messages, also must be understood. If the micro is being considered solely for the purpose of implementing EMS, a company may not want to invest this much training time and effort. Software-based EMS generally requires more attention and monitoring from the user than the hardware-based systems.

Status indicators—whether a screen line or other type—are of less importance with EMS software than with the hardware-based systems, since the program is generally quite self-contained and needs little input from the user. The lack of any kind of concurrent operation means that whatever function is being performed will be obvious from the screen, and will probably have been initiated by the user.

Integration with Other Operations

The use of the microcomputer as a communications terminal has both advantages and disadvantages in terms of integrating it with other office operations. As mentioned previously, EMS software may permit transmission of any disk file including spreadsheets, graphics and programs. The data can thus be shared and used by many people without having to be reformatted. While this results in duplicated files—and is not as sophisticated as the file sharing permitted by a local area network—it certainly is preferable to recreating the files for each user, and is both faster and safer than transporting floppy disks. On the other hand, while it facilitates integration, this type of system may cause line contention problems and may also create overdependence on one piece of equipment.

The level and ease of integration of the message system with word processing operations will depend on the use of compatible software to create and read the files, but it can be achieved. Integration with other office operations, such as the voice telephone system or other non-DDD data networks probably cannot be achieved through these software products, at least not yet. Personal appointment calendars are incorporated into some systems, which is useful if there is only one user at a site.

EMS SOFTWARE FOR LOCAL AREA NETWORKS

The most advanced microcomputer EMS software comes closest to offering the range of EMS capabilities provided by CBM services when it is incorporated into a LAN. Microcomputer LANs are a type of hybrid system, since they are neither strictly software nor strictly hardware based, but rather, incorporate elements of both. LAN products may be designed for a specific type of microcomputer (Vector Graphic's MaiLINC is an example) or may be compatible with several types (LAN: Mail Monitor runs on Apple, IBM and Corvus hardware). These products handle all of the desirable mail functions, and offer the advantage of having excellent integration with other office functions.

Local area networks, of course, are primarily hard-wired systems connecting users within a single building or campus environment. Although the microcomputer LANs use distributed rather than centralized processing, their functions (especially in terms of EMS) are more apt to resemble in-house minicomputer or mainframe networks.

LANs may or may not provide links to external communications networks; the links may not offer all of the features of the internal LAN mail system.

EMS SOFTWARE PACKAGES

A number of EMS software packages for microcomputers and microcomputer LANs are described below. (Addresses and telephone numbers for the manufacturers listed can be found in Appendix B.) All prices are as of 1984 and should be used for comparison only. Again, readers are urged to contact vendors for the most up-to-date information.

Specific program features and characteristics are compared on Table 8.1, page 117.

Microcom

Micro/Courier is a file exchange software package for Apple and IBM microcomputers. Using DDD lines, and with identical systems at either end, it can perform unattended transfer of any type of files. The software provides a directory of up to 99 mailboxes or addresses. Mailboxes can be grouped into mailing lists. The clock/calendar controls automatic dialing; blocked calls are redialed up to 10 times. Incoming files are stored on disk, with a record of date, time, sender, file name and other identifying information. Up to four disk drives can be supported to allow for high message traffic needs. The software incorporates a terminal mode, which will allow the micro to access other computer systems.

Price: $150

Software Connections, Inc.

The LAN: Mail Monitor is a store-and-forward message and file transfer system for use on the Corvus Omninet local area network. In this configuration it can connect Apple II/IIe, IBM and Corvus Concept microcomputers into an integrated network. Messages can be sent internally over the LAN or over telephone lines. A standard letter format is provided; messages and files can also be transferred from a compatible word processing program. Distribution lists are offered, and confirmation of message receipt is provided. Password protection ensures privacy. Two versions support up to 25 or up to 10,000 users, respectively. A designated "Postmaster" personal computer station controls modem-sharing and printer-sharing for the network.

Price: $745 to $1195

Transend Corp.

Transend/PC is a software package for IBM microcomputers that supports automatic log-on, transmittal and tracking of messages to other micros. Screen "baskets" handle message composition, addressing and transmitting, as well as personal calendars and other files. Transend 3 offers similar features for Apple computers.

Price: $189

Table 8.1: Comparison of Microcomputer EMS Software

Feature	MaiLINC	Postman	SofGram
Messaging			
Header with time/date	x		x
with sender/recipient	x		x
with subject heading	x		
Multiple recipients	x	x	x
Message forwarding	x		x
Message cancelling			x
Message acknowledgment	x	x	x
List incoming mail		x	x
List outgoing mail		x	x
Save received or sent mail	x	x	x
File Storage			
Private files			x
Shared (designated access)	x		x
Public (unrestricted access)			x
Message/File Retrieval			
By date			
By sender/recipient			x
By subject			x
By system assigned number		x	
Bulletin Board			
Conferencing			
Online "chatting" (two users)			
Conference (three or more users)			
Text Manipulation			
Line editor			
Formatting (paging, etc.)		x	
Full screen editor			x
User Aids			
Menus/command prompting	x	x	x
Online help instructions	x	x	x
User defined forms			x
Delivery Options			
Outdial to user terminal		x	
Direct telex/TWX		x	x
First class mail		x	

(Table 8.1 continued on next page)

Table 8.1: (cont.)

Feature	MaiLINC	Postman	SofGram
Mailgram		x	x
Interconnect to other EMS			
Communications Networks			
Public telephone (dial-up DDD)		x	x
Private telephone (leased line)			
Telex, TWX		x	x
LAN, coaxial cable	x		
LAN, twisted pair cable			
Transmission Speeds			
50 bps			
110 bps			x
300 bps		x	x
1200 bps		x	x
2400 bps or higher	x		
Ports Available			
Communications lines (maximum)	NA	1	NA
User I/O stations (maximum)	NA	1	NA

Vector Graphics, Inc.*

The MaiLINC software is a messaging package for use on local area networks using the Vector 4 series of microcomputers. The mailbox system allows for password security if desired, and supports both mailbox-to-mailbox and group distribution of messages. Operations are simplified by the use of menus and function keys. The Vector Graphics LAN uses twisted-pair wire.

Price: $995

COMMUNICATING WORD PROCESSORS

Communicating word processors (CWPs) are another type of hybrid EMS product, since they incorporate both specialized software and hardware modifications to the equipment itself.

*Product appears in the comparison chart given in Table 8.1.

Early Word Processing Equipment

Word processing equipment was introduced into the marketplace in the early 1970s. Intended for the handling of correspondence and document creation, it was viewed as a high-powered typewriter. Early word processors were mainly stand-alone units, having all the necessary capabilities in a single workstation.

Since the primary focus of word processors is on the production of letter-quality printed output, the printer is a major cost factor in a word processor installation. To reduce this cost, and to enable distribution of workstations more widely throughout an organization, systems were designed to share a single high-quality printer. In a typical configuration, the single printer would be shared by up to three workstations, with the capability to queue up to six printing jobs at a time. Communications capability allowing each stand-alone unit to exchange data with the others in these small clusters was developed to support these installations. However, not every stand-alone word processor can be configured into such a cluster arrangement, and many cannot support a communications capability.

Stand-alone word processors range in cost from $7000 to $13,000, with the units at the low end generally offering more limited storage and display capabilities as well as more rudimentary printing.

Shared Logic Word Processors

Another category of word processing equipment is designed for incorporation into a larger network, with central processing and storage to support a number of workstations. In such a shared-resource system, the logic and processing functions are performed by a central processing unit, and a large number of terminals can be supported. Most of these systems can provide for an average of 14 printers and 16 workstations. Installations of this type of system have dominated the market for word processing equipment in the 1980s.

The significance of the emergence of such shared resource systems is that this type of system, by its nature, must possess data communications capability to allow each workstation to communicate with the central processor. With this capability present, it is easy for each workstation to communicate with others. Shared logic systems supporting a large number of terminals tend to be distributed more widely throughout an office, making workstations available to more personnel.

These systems are generally more expensive than the stand-alone units, costing between $13,000 and $20,000. Such units are generally practical for large organizations, where there is a need to support and link more than three or four word processors.

EMS SOFTWARE FOR COMMUNICATING WORD PROCESSORS

While most word processing equipment vendors are now offering communications capability for linking workstations, this alone is not the equivalent of electronic mail. Basic communications support is likely to provide only the capability to access the same files on a central facility, or to send a document from one workstation to another.

True electronic mail capability requires additional software for the word processing system, providing the type of mailbox, message storage and message retrieval services that have been described earlier for CBMS systems. There are two ways in which this can be achieved using word processors. The first is to run an electronic mail system using the shared central processing unit installed for the word processing system. An example of this type of service is Wang's Mailway message network. This system is available in three different versions, ranging from a very simple point-to-point document delivery system (Level 1), to a sophisticated user-progammable system (Level 3) that provides mail delivery to individual mailboxes, and is accessible from various types of workstations.

The second way to use word processing equipment for electronic mail is to install terminal emulation software. This software allows the workstations to be used as terminals for accessing remote CBMS systems. This has the advantage of using the word processor's capabilities to create and edit documents locally. These documents and messages can then be transmitted to remote sites by dialing into the CBMS and transferring the text. Depending on local software capabilities, it may also be possible to transfer incoming messages and documents into the word processor for local storage and revision. An example of this type of remote access package is the NCR Worksaver Electronic Mail Interface for NCR word processing equipment. This interface allows the NCR workstation to emulate a terminal (appropriately configured for accessing the ITT Dialcom electronic mail system); provides a menu-driven interface, which prompts the user through the selection of the mail function; and facilitates the transfer of files from the CWP to the remote CBMS.

Installed CWP Base

There is still a large base of installed word processors that do not have communications capability. In some cases, a simple software installation—along with the attachment of a modem or other link to a communications network—will provide the added capability, but not every word processor can be upgraded in this fashion. Some units which are so equipped are nevertheless not used for communicating. In fact, as of June 1983, only 30% of installed word processors were estimated to have a communications function, and only a third of those were believed to be effectively used for communications in the work environment.[2]

Despite these statistics, the communicating word processor has emerged as an important factor in office communications. Many businesses now purchasing word processing equipment identify communications capability as one of the most important features to be considered in selecting the equipment. It is expected that by 1985, all word processors leaving the manufacturer should be equipped for communications.[3]

SUMMARY

As noted, the software microcomputer EMS products are most suitable for low message traffic environments where the lack of simultaneous access by several users or to multiple communications lines is not a problem. The geographic dispersal of the network is usually regionalized, since the use of only the DDD network for transcontinental or international traffic is not as cost-effective as other networks. All of these characteristics also apply to communicating word processors and the microcomputer LANs.

For a single-station microcomputer or word processor, there are other advantages: implementation costs are low (the hardware may already be in place), the software is not expensive, installation can be done by the user and extensive training is not required. The ability to use the same equipment for a wide variety of non-EMS functions enhances the economic appeal of these systems, even while it increases the possibility that demand for access to the equipment may create bottlenecks. However, even if the system is "outgrown" for EMS, the equipment does not become obsolete for other functions. This last factor alone may sway users who want to "ease into" EMS.

It should be kept in mind that there is very little to prevent a single microcomputer or word processor from expanding into a full LAN installation in the future. This makes hybrid products extremely attractive.

FOOTNOTES

1. Myron Berger, "Message for Owners of PCs: Modem links you to Telex" *Wall Street Computer Review*, (September/October 1983):69.

2. M. Hayward, "The WP Solution," *Computerworld* 17 (16A) (April 20, 1983): 49-51.

3. "A Year of Living Uncertainly: Outlook '84 Office Automation Systems," *Modern Office Technology* 29(1) (January 1984): 42-44.

9

Interconnection Services: The Outside Link

The variety of available electronic mail services increases every day, as new software packages, equipment and CBMS services proliferate. The inevitable problem, with such a diversity of alternatives to choose from, is selecting the appropriate option from among all possible candidates. In many cases, it may not be a matter of selecting the one right choice, but rather of determining the optimal combination of services to meet internal and external communications requirements.

Regardless of which system is chosen for internal communications, it will be necessary to deal with a wide variety of services and systems if communication with other organizations is intended or required. Interconnection services fulfill this need. Interconnection services are essentially add-on services, used to fill out an organization's external communications needs. They may also be appropriate for organizations that do not have much internal electronic mail activity, but do communicate with diverse organizations.

NEED FOR INTERCONNECTION SERVICES

The need for interconnection services is the inevitable result of the uncontrolled environment in which electronic mail has developed. Rather than a single, universal service, such as is provided by government supported mail delivery, organizations must choose from a variety of commercial vendors, whose systems are generally not compatible.

Lack of Universality

Most electronic mail vendors and users have approached the implementation of mail service on an organizational basis. For example, an organization can use the same computer system that provides administrative and accounting support to implement an EMS software package for internal messaging. As a result, in this case EMS is limited to internal users. In another scenario, a microcomputer network is implemented on a local area network (LAN), accessible only to those connected to that local link.

Even the use of an external commercial service does not necessarily widen the universe outside the organization. Most vendors sell CBMS services for use by members of a single organization—and even though there are other organizations, customers or suppliers using the same CBMS, there is often no central directory to make them known to each other.

Thus, while all of these approaches are valid ways to improve the efficiency of internal communications, they all suffer equally from an inability to support external communications. At the present time, the public TWX/telex network is still the most universal form of electronic communication, and that network cannot deliver a message to any recipient unless that person has a public telex number.

Multiple Independent Systems

The existence of many different services makes it unlikely that all of the people or organizations with whom you wish to communicate can be reached on one system. Until such time as one electronic mail service becomes the predominant choice, many organizations will be faced with the necessity of dealing with several different electronic mail systems. For example, a retail outlet is likely to be offered the opportunity for electronic ordering and communication with major suppliers through its EMS—but each supplier is likely to choose a different EMS for the purpose. Of course, this problem has not gone unrecognized, and several services have emerged that attempt to fill the gap.

SOLVING THE INTERCONNECTION PROBLEM

There are three general kinds of alternatives available to companies or individuals requiring communications capabilities with multiple vendors or services. These alternatives can be loosely described as software solutions, hardware solutions and service solutions. The characteristics of the software and hardware options were described in previous chapters and are reviewed here only for comparison to the subject of this chapter: interconnection.

Software

Software solutions to the problem of communicating with users of several different communications services are attractive to the end user because of the presence of local control and consistency in the user interface. With the more sophisticated software packages, the ability to tailor or customize the package to individual requirements can be significant. The Transend product (described in Chapter 8) is an example of a software package that allows the user to tailor the communications program to work transparently with multiple electronic mail systems. By creating software capable of automatically logging on and interacting with several different CBMS services, Transend enables the user to create messages offline and send them to electronic mailboxes, literally at the touch of a button.

Drawbacks

While providing significant advantages to the user, there are certain drawbacks to the software solution. One complication is that the user must have accounts, mailboxes, passwords and bills from several systems. As the number of services used grows, managing multiple invoices may become increasingly confusing—rather like being billed separately for phone calls to individual cities. The analogy is an accurate one in that a group of EMS users on the same system comprise a virtual community in electronic space.

Another drawback of software solutions to the problem of multiple communications services results from the wide variations in user interface protocols among EMS services and networks. Some EMS services are primarily prompt-driven or require the use of a menu to select each command. Other systems are command-driven, with a sparse vocabulary that seems to assume the user is another computer, rather than a human being.

These differences in presentation, which often determine whether a service is characterized by the term "user-friendly" or not, also have an impact on how "computer-friendly" an electronic mail system is and how well it will respond to instructions from a communications software package. Not just communications protocols, but also message formatting, addressing, routing and confirmation conventions vary from system to service. Telex requires a different basic set of operator information and instructions than CBMS.

Future Improvements

New features are constantly being developed and implemented on virtually all electronic mail services. As the range of choices expands and the capabilities of electronic mail services are enhanced over the next years, present software packages will become obsolete and will require revision and updating to remain useful and competitive. Progressively more sophisticated local software will be required to manage the network capability that will be available.

Until the arrival of the controversial "fifth generation" of technology, imbued with true artificial intelligence, communications software packages will not be flexible enough to provide a completely transparent service to every EMS system or network.

Hardware

Hardware solutions have similar drawbacks and are more expensive to implement. Using a special piece of equipment to communicate with multiple systems is most common in two kinds of applications: those requiring interconnection with both synchronous and asynchronous networks, and within large-scale or specialized communications centers. The first kind of application is most often encountered in local area network environments and the second in corporate message centers. In any case, fairly large message traffic volume is required to make multi-functional stand-alone communications equipment cost-effective.

Intelligent modems, equipped with microprocessors and solid-state storage, are important communications peripherals. As solutions to the interconnection problem, intelligent modems still require the user to establish the connections with multiple systems and to program the device(s). Users must still subscribe to the various systems or services they wish to communicate with.

It is likely that prospective users of electronic mail will already know if their application requires specialized hardware to implement. As with so many other aspects of the telecommunications industry, the technology is changing quickly and new products are constantly being introduced to fill emerging requirements and satisfy new applications.

Interconnection Services

The third approach to obtaining general-purpose communications capabilities is to use the interconnection facilities provided by a service or network. Until recently, the network interconnections available to users were very limited. It has only been in the last decade that even TWX and telex users have been able to communicate with each other. This is not surprising considering the difference in technology, coding structure, protocol and speed between the TWX and telex systems. The fact that these systems were also competitive offerings did not help the cause of interconnection.

The development of CBMS over the last 15 years occurred without benefit of long-term planning or coordination, in some cases as a by-product of other projects. As electronic mail systems have matured into service offerings from timesharing service bureaus and information utilities, EMS capabilities have been continuously refined. No longer ancillary to other products, electronic mail has become a primary focus for many companies attempting to stake out their territory in the lucrative office automation market.

Recognizing that the ability to transmit messages to a wider audience will result in increased use of EMS services, some of the CBMS vendors are beginning to provide the user with interconnections to other communication services. OnTyme, Dialcom, EasyLink and Telemail users can all send messages to the telex network. Some EMS users may send mailgrams and telegrams. In most of these electronic mail services, the user is given another program, external to the regular electronic mail service, that is used for formatting and sending other kinds of messages. In a few systems the user may be able to receive inbound messages from telex or other networks, although true bi-directional interconnections are rare.

Currently, there are two types of interconnection services that are used for EMS: hybrid services, which combine electronic transmission with hard-copy delivery, and gateway services, which provide a link between differing electronic systems. The major types of services available in each of these categories are described below. (Addresses and phone numbers for the vendors mentioned can be found in Appendix B.)

HYBRID SERVICES: PRIORITY MAIL INTERCONNECTIONS

The most common form of electronic mail service interconnection is a link from a CBMS to one of the variety of priority mail systems. There are many forms of priority mail service available, including courier and package delivery services, Special Delivery and Express Mail services from the post office, and that oldest form of priority mail, the message that started the electronic mail revolution nearly 150 years ago, the telegram.

For the purposes of this book, priority mail services are defined as hard-copy message delivery systems that accept input in machine-readable form which is then printed and delivered, most commonly through the local first class mail system. (They should not be confused with the U.S. Postal Service designation "priority mail," which simply refers to large packages delivered as first class mail.) Since priority mail services are, in fact, only half electronic mail, they represent a hybrid form of EMS service. Several available services are examined more closely below.

Mailgrams

The Mailgram is a priority mail offering from Western Union (WU). Machine-readable messages are sent to a WU telex or DDD number, delivered to special printing facilities and then placed into first class mail. Mailgram service is both well-established and generally reliable, with next-day delivery available in most cities within the United States.

The Source introduced an interconnection service to Western Union, allowing messages to be delivered to a recipient in paper format as a Mailgram. Other services followed suit, and many commercial CBMS services now offer this capability.

The Computer Letter is a cousin of the Mailgram. Also a service of Western Union, Computer Letters are similar to Mailgrams in the way they are input, have either one or two-day delivery times, and are printed on uniform stationery (i.e., organizations cannot use their own letterhead, add logos, etc.). Computer Letters are priced by the page, unlike Mailgrams which are priced by the number of words contained in the message. Western Union is the only electronic mail vendor that currently provides a Computer Letter link.

E-COM

The U.S. Postal Service announced its electronic communications service in 1982. E-COM (Electronic Computer Originated Mail) is not an electronic mail service in the sense defined in this book; like the mailgrams discussed above, it is a hybrid service. E-COM allows text created on a local computer or word processor to be transmitted electronically to a designated post office (there are 25 post offices currently accepting E-COM). At the post office, the messages are printed (up to two pages), folded, placed in envelopes and delivered in the first class mail.

E-COM messages are supposed to be delivered in two days or less, which is a significant improvement over regular first class delivery. However, the direct use of E-COM requires a minimum of 200 pieces per transmission, prepayment of postage costs and use of a fairly complex formatting control language. In addition, E-COM messages print without letterhead or signature, making them inappropriate for some business applications.

Since its inception, the service has been a highly controversial one, prompting criticism from private industry and plagued with lower than expected revenues and volume. In June 1984 the board of governors of the Postal Service voted to abandon the E-COM service, and turn it over to a private firm, if possible.[1]

MCI Mail

In fall 1983, a new general electronic mail service aimed at serving primarily the business user was introduced. MCI, with a nationwide communications network already in place for the support of long-distance telephone service, announced its entry into the field with a major promotional campaign. MCI Mail attempts to provide both CBMS-type electronic mail service and universal delivery capability in hard-copy as needed.

If the intended recipient is not an online MCI user, the message is printed out at an MCI Mail service center and placed into first class mail for delivery. Although similar in some respects to E-COM, MCI Mail is offering the user an option to send a laser-printed logo and signature, creating a facsimile of company letterhead.

GATEWAY INTERCONNECTION SERVICES

A full service interconnection capability requires the transfer of messages not only from electronic system to hard copy delivery, but also from one EMS to another. Such multi-level interconnection is available through service bureaus providing direct interconnection to several electronic mail systems through a standard user interface. These services are often referred to as "gateways."

A gateway provides the conversion of transmission protocols and message formats necessary to switch a message from one system to another. Most gateway services are capable of transferring to or from only a few specific types of formats, and will therefore only partially solve the problems of universality defined above. As with EMS services, however, gateways are becoming increasingly more sophisticated. Some of the existing gateway interconnection services are described below.

Graphnet

Graphnet offers the Freedom network, which provides transfer of messages created on a standard computer terminal into the TWX or telex networks. The user interface is through a standard DDD connection to the Graphnet computer, which allows the user to create a message and enter the desired TWX/telex number. Graphnet will then dial the TWX/telex number, and transmit the message with the necessary protocol conversion to the desired TWX or telex network.

The basic service is a real-time connection—Graphnet links directly to the TWX/telex machine, requiring that the recipient's machine be available to receive a message at that particular moment. However, Graphnet also offers a store-and-forward capability, providing a mailbox in which the message can be stored while the connection is being made. This allows Graphnet to handle the redialing automatically if the TWX/telex number is busy.

EasyLink

Western Union is now offering its own version of a CBMS service with elements of gateway capability. EasyLink allows the user to access the service using a standard computer terminal and DDD connection. The message is then converted to TWX/telex protocol and sent to the designated machine.

Like Graphnet, EasyLink provides for automatic redialing if the receipent's machine is busy. EasyLink has no text editing capabilities; it is most useful for transfer of messages already created on an in-house word processor or computer to another mailbox or a telex number. EasyLink is being sold as a CBMS service with an option for telex. Users selecting the telex option pay an additional monthly service charge and are then able to send telex messages to numbers in the Western Union TWX/telex network.

Delphi

Delphi, a service of General Videotex, offers services specifically aimed at the home microcomputer owner. In addition to bulletin boards, banking, online chatting, shopping and games, the system offers a standard interface to a few other host computer systems, including Dialcom and Dialog Information Services, Inc.

This type of gateway service offers relatively little protocol conversion, since the service merely facilitates the log-on process to other hosts. Once logged on to one of the other host systems, the user is interacting directly with that system, and must use that host system's command language. Delphi does not provide a mechanism for actually transferring a message from one host to another, but rather provides an entry path to other hosts.

ITT/Dialcom

Dialcom provides a CBMS service with the basic features listed in Chapter 4. In addition, Dialcom also provides gateway capabilities, so that other types of online services can be accessed while connected to Dialcom. This service, called Infogate, allows the user to select desired online systems with a one-word command from a menu. The gateway software then initiates the connection to the selected remote system, so that the user does not have to establish a separate telecommunications link for each separate service. Once connected, the user must complete the regular log-on procedures. The user must establish separate accounts with each online service to be accessed.

Information retrieved from the various systems can then be stored in a workspace on the Dialcom system and redistributed to others via the electronic mail facility. This provides a rudimentary capability for transferring messages and data from one system to another.

International Electronic Mail Service

International Electronic Mail Service (IEMS) offers a set of services specifically designed to solve the interconnection problem. IEMS is an independent corporation, holding agency agreements with two of the world's largest international record carriers, Western Union and ITT World Communications. IEMS also works closely with Tymshare Corp. in the resale of the OnTyme electronic mail service. IEMS sells electronic mailboxes that have been augmented to allow the user to send and receive messages with users of many other systems and services.

IEMS uses the capabilities of OnTyme, ITT, Western Union and other communication networks to preprocess and format messages as much as possible. IEMS provides a type of virtual communications processor that resides within other networks and uses the facilities of other networks combined with the hardware and software of the IEMS operations center. Users consult a service menu to send messages that can be switched to TWX, telex, priority mail or another designated CBMS service. At present, IEMS can be used to transfer messages among EasyLink, Dialcom, OnTyme, TWX, telex and MCI, as well as to send many types of priority mail.

Any terminal and modem can be used to access the user's mailbox over the DDD network in the United States and Canada, or other countries supporting DDD transmission. IEMS customers may also use any telex or TWX machine for this purpose. In many parts of the world it is neither easy nor inexpensive to connect a terminal for DDD transmission. In some countries, turning a telex machine into a computer terminal is the only way to obtain access to computer hosts.

IEMS implements interconnection and communications services on a network level whenever possible. Message traffic that cannot be handled by the networks is forwarded to specialized communications processors in the IEMS operations center. A professional communications staff attends to messages that cannot be processed by network or automated techniques.

ADVANTAGES OF INTERCONNECTION SERVICES

Interconnection services offer significant advantages for many communications applications. As with most other aspects of communications, the particular requirements of a company's (or individual's) application will determine the relevance and importance of interconnection capabilities.

A basic function of interconnection services is the provision of a link to networks and services the user may not otherwise be able to reach. Interconnection services can solve the problem of communicating with a recipient who uses incompatible equipment or service.

The standard interface is also an important feature of an interconnection service. Whether handled by clerical staff or by senior management, communications services should be both easy to use and difficult to abuse. It should be as difficult as possible for a communications attempt to fail. The standard interface provided by an interconnection service can be an enormous benefit in many applications. By using a single system, service and set of message formatting conventions, the interconnection service can reduce confusion and frustration.

Another advantage of interconnection services is the simplification of communications management. An interconnection service is responsible not only for the communications protocol, any conversions and interface, but also for the billing. The interconnection agency coordinates and rebills service from multiple vendors. The user receives a single bill with itemized accounting for all electronic communications. A single communications invoice that summarizes electronic communications costs by department and message is useful to companies that rely on several types of communications services to transact their business.

An interconnection service also provides the user with a link to services that may be otherwise unavailable without a special ID and log-on protocol. The interconnection service eliminates the need to subscribe to multiple services and to keep up with the many changes and enhancements being introduced by the various communications vendors.

In sum, until the implementation of a truly universal electronic mail service, the interconnection service provides the best alternative for users who wish to broaden the scope of their EMS activities. Unlike software and hardware solutions to the problem of interorganizational communications, interconnection services undertake the maintenance of user and machine-friendly interface protocol and formatting. Further, users are assured of service that evolves with the state-of-the-art in communications technology. A user is neither expected nor required to keep up with the constantly changing communications environment outside of local needs. The task is delegated to another agency that performs the job for many clients at the same time.

FOOTNOTES

1. *New York Times*, "Computer Mail Effort Abandoned" (New York, June 6, 1984).

10

Future Trends for Electronic Mail

There is no doubt that the era of electronic communications has arrived with the 1980s, and that electronic mail is a vital part of it. The maturation of data communications technology, the availability of intelligent workstations in the office and the need for improved efficiency in business communications are some of the factors that are already bringing about the increasing use of electronic mail.

But there are many questions as yet unresolved. Will there ever be a national electronic mail system comparable to the national postal system? Will electronic mail facilitate international communications or will diverging technical standards make worldwide communications more difficult? Will it be possible for businesses to install systems that integrate all communications—voice, text, video and graphics—into one coherent communications system, or will different vendors dominate each area of technology? And will individual use of electronic mail for personal correspondence ever become the norm?

Previous chapters have provided an introduction to the major options for implementation of electronic mail service, and a basis for comparison of the various characteristics of these service options. All of these options are services that are currently available and operate within existing technology. But these chapters do not pin down and definitively describe electronic mail. As with most areas of modern life, EMS is constantly changing. Just as there are many service capabilities described in this book that were not available or economically feasible even two years ago, there are new services springing up which may make the current options obsolete in two more years.

Many forces will affect the future development and availability of electronic mail. Some are technological capabilities, some are socioeconomic factors and some may be unpredictable "wild card" events like the deregulation of AT&T (see below). This final chapter will explore some of the issues of EMS, touching on the events and significant developments in EMS services that will influence the use of electronic mail. This chapter will also provide some reflections on the questions listed above and on future trends for electronic mail.

AT&T DIVESTITURE

A major event that unfolded during the time this book was written was the deregulation of AT&T and the concomitant divestiture of the local telephone companies. Although divestiture officially took place as of January 1984, the actual impact of this change will probably not be fully felt until sometime in 1985, as the newly-formed regional phone companies work out new rate schedules for local service with the FCC. Although no one can predict just what will happen, it is possible that the cost of services such as TWX/telex, which require a local loop installation, will skyrocket. Increased cost of local phone service may also make the economics of local area networks and local PBX services increasingly attractive.

Meanwhile, AT&T is likely to lower long-distance phone rates, which may make significant changes in the economics of packet-switched networks and in the cost of supplying broadband, high-speed data communications. The overall implications of this constellation of events makes comparison of EMS services according to the current rates for various telecommunications services almost useless, since these will certainly be significantly changed by the end of 1984. That is one reason why cost comparisons have not been emphasized in this book.

No matter what the long-term results, telephone company divestiture is probably the single most important factor to be considered and watched during 1984. It will surely affect both the technical and economic environment for EMS services.

FAILURE OF E-COM

The E-COM service offered by the U.S. Postal Service (USPS) was among the interconnection services described in Chapter 9. The Postal Service's decision to abandon E-COM in June 1984 has some interesting lessons for both the USPS and the commercial electronic mail sector.

Drawbacks to E-COM

There were several drawbacks to the E-COM service. The rigidity and unattractiveness of the format, lack of letterhead and signature, and high volume requirements in pricing were all factors contributing to the lack of enthusiasm with which E-COM was received by those who decide how to deliver mail within the business community. In addition, E-COM received negative publicity because of concerns about government subsidy and competition with the private sector.

The USPS claims that use of electronic technology is essential to its survival as an economically viable service. But a hybrid service like E-COM, which merely facilitated the use of regular mail delivery and did not offer any of the message control and handling functions of a full-fledged EMS service, lacked sufficient attraction to make the USPS a significant force in electronic mail. In addition, E-COM faced increasing competition from the commercial sector. For example, the MCI service, introduced in fall 1983, provides the capability for first class mail delivery along with a CBMS service. With reproduction of letterhead and signatures available, MCI solved some of the problems of E-COM.

The USPS and Electronic Mail

It will be a long time before competing electronic delivery methods make serious inroads into USPS business. In 1983, EMS accounted for less than 1% of all mail in the U.S., and it is not likely to represent more than 2% before 1987, based on projections of more than 2 billion pieces of electronically delivered mail in 1987.[1] Nevertheless, to date, the USPS has been unable to compete electronically, and other services can be expected to skim off the profit cream of this part of the market. In the long run, the USPS will have to redefine its investment in electronic service. The long-term solution may be some kind of cooperative interrelationship with the commercial services.

GRAPHIC AND VISUAL TRANSMISSION SERVICES

Although current EMS services are oriented toward text transmission, the capability to transmit graphics, pictures and visual images will be an important trend of future EMS services. Major types of graphics services are described below.

Facsimile Services

Facsimile communication (fax) allows the sender to transmit documents without rekeying and with graphic images such as signatures. Facsimile will become a more important factor in the overall communications industry because of technological changes which have recently occurred and others which can be expected in 1984 and 1985.

Introduction of Standards

The establishment of standards for facsimile transmission by the International Telephone and Telegraph Consultative Committee (CCITT) is beginning to transform fax into a competitive technology. The recently introduced Group III facsimile machines, based on a standard for digital transmission, permit much faster transmission than with earlier equipment. Further, Group III machines are able to communicate with each other regardless of manufacturer. This technology should soon replace the older analog technology for fax, which suffers from slow transmission speeds and a lack of compatibility among manufacturers.

As digital fax equipment becomes more common, there will probably be an expansion in the use of fax because of the broader universe of compatible machines and higher transmission speeds of 20 to 30 seconds per page. An even faster generation of machines, capable of operating at transmission speeds of five seconds per page, is not far from reality. With higher speeds, fax becomes truly feasible as a document delivery medium. Federal Express, one of the major suppliers of courier services, introduced a facsimile-based delivery service in mid-1984, using equipment produced by the Nippon Electric Co. Federal Express hopes to displace as much as 60% of its air freight traffic volume to fax service.

Integration of Systems

State-of-the-art facsimile equipment can be integrated with some existing computer networks. For example, the Xerox Telecopier 495-I includes RS-232 communications ports and is capable of transferring data directly from storage in an in-house computer system to a remote fax machine. Such integrated systems will make it easier to justify the purchase of facsimile equipment.

Fax-based EMS Services

A number of fax-based services are emerging. One, offered by Mail Boxes, Etc., is aimed at small business users without in-house fax equipment. Clients are offered walk-in fax service at franchises in 18 states, and transmitted text is either held for pick-up, mailed or read to the recipient over the phone. There are also several fax interconnection services. ITT now offers Faxpak, which provides value added facsimile transmission. Among other capabilities, Faxpak allows input from telex units and ASCII terminals to be transmitted to fax machines, by translating the coded characters into a pattern representing a visual image. Graphnet is another character-to-image translation service allowing terminals to interact with fax machines.

International Fax Services

International fax services are available through several agencies, including ITT's Worldfax service, Western Union International Facsimile Services and RCA Global Communications Inc.'s Q-FAX. Transmissions can be originated by dialing in from the user's fax equipment to the chosen host network (walk-in service is available in certain U.S. cities) and then forwarded to offices located in principal cities of foreign countries. The U.S. Postal Service offers another alternative for international fax through Intelpost. Documents can be delivered to the Intelpost service points in Washington, DC and New York, and from that point transmitted by fax to cooperating PTTs for local delivery. The rates and the countries covered by the various international fax services vary significantly, but service is available to Canada, many European countries, Japan, Australia and Argentina.

Greenfield Information Services has announced plans to publish a directory of facsimile users (scheduled for late 1984), which will list phone numbers and compatibility information for facsimile machines located in a number of corporations which have agreed to participate.[2] The existence of directories of this type will make it possible for facsimile to be used not only for internal communications, but as a general communications vehicle.

Optical Character Recognition

While not truly a technology that supports graphics, optical character recognition (OCR) is an alternative data entry method to the keyboarding of text, and presents an interesting potential for transmission of documents that already exist in typed or printed form. Employing scanning equipment which "reads" a page of text and translates each character into its digital equivalent, this type of input can be as much as 50 times faster than manual keying at a workstation. Today's scanners can input 300 pages per hour—versus the six to 10 pages per hour than can be input by a typist—at a fraction of the cost and more accurately. Text translated in this fashion can then be transmitted through any type of EMS, including telex, TWX, communicating word and data processors and computer networks.

OCR systems can resolve input bottlenecks in electronic mail systems where transmission of lengthy printed documents is required. However, OCR does have some significant limitations. The text must be printed or typed in a character font for which the equipment is designed. Unusual type fonts or imperfections in printing will cause scanning errors. OCR equipment cannot translate handwritten text.

The U.S. Postal Service also plans to use OCR to streamline the processing of first class mail. For mail to be processed by such equipment, it will have to meet certain size standards, and the printing must be OCR-readable. Thus, business correspondence will have to adhere to certain addressing formats in order to take advantage of this new technology.

Videotex

Videotex is an online, interactive service for accessing computer systems. It allows the display of pages of text and graphic materials, usually via an encoding device hooked up to a television and connected to a computer by telephone or cable. However, the graphics display quality is of fairly low resolution and is most suited for charts, graphs and outline formats.

Types of Videotex Systems

Most of the development of videotex has been outside the U.S. Telidon was introduced in 1978 in Canada. It featured higher quality graphics than the Prestel videotex introduced somewhat earlier in Great Britain. Telidon's alpha-geometric technique of graphic-information encoding is suited for use in both one-way broadcast (teletext) and two-way broadcast (videotex) systems. The Telidon presentation level code is of particular interest because it has been taken as the basis for AT&T videotex services.

As with other alternative communications protocols, the most pressing question remaining for the future of videotex is that of standards. Although AT&T is working with the Telidon protocol, IBM's videotex system is based on Prestel.

Future of Videotex in the U.S. Market

It is not yet clear whether videotex has any place in the U.S. business environment. Since so many businesses already use computers and automated office systems to handle database services and electronic mail, videotex may be redundant.

However, there may be room for videotex in the consumer market. There are some predictions that videotex will become as common as the television set in the average household, allowing the home user to send electronic mail, obtain information on a wide variety of subjects and perform various transaction-based services such as home banking and home shopping. Indeed, a number of videotex trials were initiated in the U.S. in 1983.

As of mid-1984, however, videotex is available only in very limited areas in the U.S. The success of videotex may be linked to the spread of cable TV, since some cable systems provide the capability to use the cable network for data communications. In terms of home use of electronic mail, videotex services, along with the consumer-oriented online systems such as The Source, offer potential for increased use during the 1980s.

Video Conferencing

Video conferencing is a two-way service that enables business people to face their counterparts in another city on wide-screen color television for live interaction. Although it has been technologically feasible since the early 1970s, such corporate video conferencing is not expected to have significant use before the mid-1980s due to the prohibitive cost. Hourly charges can range from $600 to $2400, depending on the kind of network facility and the number of conferencing points.

As the cost of travel rises rapidly in terms of money and management time, the economics of the video conference are becoming less forbidding. Significant payback can be realized just through savings on plane tickets, lodging and managers' time spent traveling. However, the real economic justification for video conferencing is through integration with other communications services.

Video communications is generally handled through satellite networks, which provide the high-speed and broad bandwidth necessary for high-quality visual display. The integration of computer-to-computer data transfer, voice communications and electronic mail on the same satellite network offers possibilities for spreading out the high initial costs of establishing a satellite link (ground stations cost about $70,000). This may make video conferencing a viable communications alternative for large organizations in the 1980s.

INTEGRATED OFFICE SYSTEMS

One trend that has already been touched up on in previous chapters is the movement toward integrated office systems. One form of integrated office system is a software package that can be run on an in-house computer. Another form is in the evolution of equipment and services offering new combinations of communications services, which might include such capabilities as video conferencing, OCR and voice communications along with data transmission.

Software Packages

"Integrated systems" has become one of the overused buzzwords of the computer industry, often applied to systems which may support multiple functions, but which are not truly integrated. For our purposes, we will accept a fairly loose definition of integration, as implying a single service, system or software package which not only supports more than one function, but allows movement from one function to another in a way that is "transparent," or at least relatively simple for the user.

There are many examples of integrated office systems. One that has received considerable attention, due to its development by the giant of the computer industry, is the IBM "Professional Office System" (PROFS). A software package designed to run on the family of IBM mainframes, PROFS supports electronic mail, calendaring, document creation and filing and an interface to word processing. Another package is the Data General "Comprehensive Electronic Office" (CEO), which includes a similar range of capabilities but also includes a more fully integrated support for graphics, economic modeling and information manipulation functions in addition to interconnection to public and local area networks.

These packages are menu-driven (and, therefore, relatively easy to use) and allow the user to switch back and forth from one function to another. Operating at high speeds in connection to in-house mainframe or mini-computers, these systems support full screen display and editing, and far more sophisticated text manipulation capabilities than any public dial-up system. Although few offices now have a terminal on every desk, systems of this type are the most likely to provide the functions which make that concept workable. In evaluating such integrated systems, the capabilities and characteristics of the electronic mail function have a high priority, but the overall ease of use of the mutiple functions will be the primary consideration.

Intelligent Telephone Systems

The union of voice and data communications is another trend that can be expected to have increasing importance. Some predict that telephone terminals will become as pervasive as ordinary telephones are today. The phone terminal typically has autodialing and phone number storage, and is a single unit with phone for voice and data communications plus a terminal display screen and keyboard.

Displayphone and Kontact are examples of telephone/computer terminals designed for executives and managers who use telephones and computer services. Northern Telecom's Displayphone is compact and can store up to 81 phone numbers, which can be indexed. The Displayphone has 6K of memory, call-back features and intercom capabilities. It is not a microcomputer but can be successfully linked with one. Mitel Corp.'s Kontact is an intelligent phone system that can send and receive electronic mail. Some versions have word processing capabilities and personal computer options. Kontact's directory can contain 200 numbers, and its memory ranges from 128K to 256K.

Voice Mail

Voice mail systems (VMS) or voice store-and-forward systems can provide a cost-effective alternative to traditional telephone answering service functions and can supplement text-based electronic mail systems. The VMS digitizes voice signals and automatically stores messages to be picked up at specified times. In the sense of offering central control for message handling, a VMS resembles a CBMS and offers some of the same advantages. The specific characteristic of storing the actual voice signal makes this service a hybrid between EMS and regular telephone service.

At present VMS is available through commercial vendors, such as Voicemail, Inc., which allow subscribers to dial in from any point on the public phone network and leave messages. It is also possible to install VMS software on certain in-house computer systems (for example, the Voicemail version is compatible with DEC equipment), thus providing VMS capability for users of an in-house or private network.

VMS technology is still fairly new, and the service has yet to become widespread. Because it complements text messaging capability, it is likely that the future will bring CBMS services that support both voice and text messaging.

PRIVATE AND LOCAL NETWORKS

Private Long-distance Networks

Following divestiture, it is expected that AT&T will offer greatly decreased rates on long-distance communications, which will make the operation of a long-distance private network more cost-effective for organizations with a geographically dispersed user base of their computer systems.

In addition to the services available from AT&T, alternate technologies for long-distance data communications will be increasingly available. For example, in the U.S., Satellite Business Systems, Inc. (SBS) has invested more than $250 million in launching private business satellites and in developing a chain of earth stations. Its purpose is to sell satellite communications networking services to companies with long-distance data transmission requirements.

With increased alternatives in technology and service providers, high-speed, broadband transmissions will be feasible on dedicated digital networks. Organizations and businesses are likely to find that the creation of a private network is a cost-effective solution for handling increased communications, especially if the network is designed to handle both voice and data transmission.

Local Networks

As noted above in the discussion of AT&T divestiture, the expected rise in the cost of local phone service is likely to cause many businesses to reexamine the way in which they support communications services. Increases in the number of in-house PBX systems, which will be installed to handle local voice and data communications, is a key trend for the future. One estimate shows savings of 10%-25% on the costs of voice traffic alone by better controls and improved routing of calls resulting from use of a PBX.[3]

Of course local area networks (LANs) are another approach to handling local communications requirements. A 1983 survey by the Yankee Group found that 40% of 2000 U.S. companies plan to install a LAN by 1985.[4] Although a technical standard for LANs is likely to emerge eventually, for the next few years a number of different and incompatible protocols will continue to vie for dominance. As LAN technology continues to mature, the capability to connect diverse equipment, for an "open network" architecture, is likely to be the major developmental thrust for all types of LAN protocols.

The integration of LANs as a data transmission vehicle with PBX systems operating as network controllers for both voice and data communication is another important trend.

SUMMARY: TRENDS IN EMS SERVICE

As is clear from the various services described in this chapter, there are two primary trends in the evolution of electronic mail services. These are integration of diverse services into services available from a single supplier or single piece of equipment, and the interconnection of mail services from different suppliers. In fact, these two concepts are overlapping, and it is sometimes difficult to identify which is the predominate factor in any particular development.

The adoption of CCITT standards for CBMS message formats, expected in 1984, presents a new basis for interconnection in that CBMS services may begin to support direct transfer of messages from one system to another. If this happens (and the adoption of standards alone does not ensure it), then one of the most pressing problems of electronic mail, the lack of universality, will be on its way to resolution.

As the microcomputer industry continues its progress, the miniaturization of computer components is bringing a generation of portable computers that allows businessmen to compose correspondence and reports while traveling, and then plug into the nearest phone booth to transmit them back to the office. Even portable devices may become outmoded as the provision of terminals in hotel rooms and airport terminals becomes more widespread.

As data transfer technology in its many forms becomes common in the office and in the home, a change in communications capability as profound as that which was initiated by the spread of the telephone can be expected. The one thing that is certain about electronic mail in the future is that it will be available in many forms, and the question to be answered will not be whether to implement, but how to choose.

CONCLUSION: THE HUMAN IMPACT OF ELECTRONIC COMMUNICATION

One of the most interesting and intractable questions about electronic mail is. . . "What does it all mean?" On a human level, on a cultural and social level, the impact of electronic communications will certainly be profound. Just as the telegraph—and later, the telex network—altered the way the world did business and saw itself, so will the general availability of low-cost electronic messaging further change our pattern of communication and the way we organize our work and our lives.

Impact on the Workplace

Volumes are being written on the impact of electronic technology and computers in the "information age." Telecommunications is merely one component of the complex new environment we are fashioning from silicon and electrons. To ignore the implications and ramifications of electronic mail would be almost as difficult as trying to predict them.

The use of priority mail services (Mailgram, Computer Letter, etc.) is increasing daily. A common use for priority mail services is the direct-mail used by many advertisers. The proliferation of machine-readable address lists combined with the communications capabilities of an interconnection service enables virtually anyone to establish a direct mail program. But as the usage of priority mail increases and becomes common in direct mail applications, will the element of "priority" be lost? When messages are perceived as junk mail their impact disappears. When communication is trivialized the information is ignored.

As electronic mail becomes prevalent in the workplace, the opportunity to implement telecommuting options for employees will seem more attractive. Already there are many firms and individuals who manage their entire business from a microcomputer and electronic mailbox.

Not only are telecommunications changing the way we do business but also the very nature of the business being done. Hardware, software and services are being rapidly introduced to satisfy communications needs. The information age is spawning new industries and requirements for electronic communications faster than any single company can currently satisfy. The information sector of the modern economy is generating more new jobs and new technologies than any other sector. Consulting, information brokering, computer utilities and online retrieval services are examples of new enterprises that require electronic communications services. Adding the hardware and software producers, distributors and service agencies, the overall contribution of communications services to the economy is increasingly significant.

Impact on Personal Communications

There are other, more subtle aspects of electronic mail that are difficult to quantify. The bulletin board services from computer utilities (The Source, CompuServe) are an electronic environment in which people can "meet" each other, establish business and contractual relationships and transact business without ever meeting each other or having any other contact. Interaction with other people is also being directly aided and changed by the Electronic Information Exchange Service (EIES) and other computer conferencing services. Although not electronic mail in the strict store-and-forward sense, the real-time interaction possible through computer conferencing is another fascinating and potentially widespread use of telecommunications technology.

The long-term implications of electronic communications include a dramatic increase in the number of connections possible among both individuals and organizations. The increasing number of potential connections or interactions is creating a completely new environment for the sharing and dissemination of information. The increase in total possible connections combined with the speed of electronic delivery makes it possible to share new ideas very rapidly, indeed, with unprecedented speed. As voice, data and graphics capabilities are implemented in integrated service offerings, the possibilities become virtually unpredictable.

Impact on Society

In the midst of these burgeoning communications possibilities there is also the option toward isolation and anonymity. CB-like code names and "handles" are used to filter communications. Using code names, whole networks are developed in which the true identities of participants are not known. Cryptic correspondence can further mask messages and information.

From telegraph to telex, telephone to teleconferencing—each of these technologies has had an impact on the cultural, social and intellectual life of our species. We started this examination of electronic mail with the observation that long-distance communications were an important aspect of the history and fabric of human civilization. We will end with another sweeping and perhaps obvious observation.

Communication by definition implies a sender and a recipient, a two-way path of potential interaction. To experience the possibilities of telecommuncations and to use the available facilities implies, therefore, that there are others with whom one wishes to communicate. For those who already feel isolated and cut out of the new electronic environment, these exciting possibilities and potentials will not be welcome. Automated electronic communications can seem both alienating and threatening to millions not fortunate enough to enjoy or afford access to current technology and services.

The broadest possible access to the new communications technology is required if the benefits are to be fully realized. The increasing diversity of electronic communications options must not, like a tower of electronic babel, be allowed to divide the species into hundreds or thousands of different dialects. If the tools do not democratize and distribute access to communication and information services, they will instead become barriers and roadblocks to human endeavor.

FOOTNOTES

1. "The Report on Electronic Mail" (Cambridge, MA: The Yankee Group, 1982).

2. For further information on *The Facsimile Users' Directory*, contact Greenfield Information Services, 551 5th Ave., New York, NY 10176.

3. David Clutterbuck, "Why Telecommunications Strategy Rings Bells in the Boardroom," *International Management* 37 (4) (April 1982): 20-23.

4. "Still Too Many Loose Connections in the Wired Office." *International Management* 38 (3) (European edition) (March 1983): 49-50.

Appendix A: Examples of EMS Usage

One of the best ways to develop an understanding of electronic mail is to talk to others who have implemented EMS. It is useful to find out why the electronic mail service was implemented, how the system was selected, what problems developed in implementation and how the system is performing in meeting the needs of the organization.

This Appendix presents three examples of how organizations have approached EMS. Each example includes a brief background description of the communications needs of the organization, a description of the EMS service chosen, details about the implementation process and some conclusions about the strengths and weaknesses of the type of service selected.

It is interesting to note that none of these examples involves the simple installation of one EMS service to perform one communications function. All involve the use of multiple systems, although the same equipment may be used to access the various systems. This is indicative of the growing complexity of the electronic communications environment and the fact that most organizations must solve a mix of communications needs and cannot address these needs individually.

USING WORD PROCESSORS ON THE TELEX NETWORK

Background

Underwriter's Laboratory (UL) performs laboratory testing for public safety. The organization has several large facilities located at considerable distance from one another throughout the United States. UL had used the public telex network on a regular basis for many years, both for internal message communications among facilities and for external messaging, via standard telex equipment. The decision to upgrade communications capabilities was made to increase efficiency and allow for added volume.

In selecting an electronic mail configuration, UL sought an approach that could accommodate message traffic of two types: 1.) high volume, direct traffic between two primary office locations in Santa Clara (CA) and Melville (NY) and 2.) general telex traffic routed into the ITT network. Utilization of existing equipment where possible was also desirable.

System Chosen

The same word processing equipment (IBM Displaywriter) was in use in both of the primary locations at the time that systems were being evaluated. By equipping both units with asynchronous, dial-up modems, UL could use this equipment for direct point-to-point communications from one site to another over regular phone lines. The telex traffic could be accommodated on the same equipment, through use of an alternative mode of access to the ITT telex network.

This alternative access mode, which was made available by ITT to broaden the base of access to the telex network, can connect via a standard asynchronous dial-up connection to a central computer facility. ITT's computer then handles the protocol conversion and routes these messages into the public telex network for delivery to the specified telex number.

The configuration chosen by UL allows the preparation of message text on the word processor, offering significant improvement in ease of preparation compared to the telex equipment. The telex equipment is no longer needed, and it is possible to drop the leased-line connection to the telex network.

The word processor also supports a level of local storage capability, avoiding redundant message keying. The high volume traffic among the primary nodes is sent direct at 1200 bps, for significant improvement in message delivery speed.

Implementation

The word processing staff was involved in the decision to implement the new communications capability. The staff was responsible for enhancing equipment, purchasing the modem and software, and staffing the message center. Each of the two primary office locations involved in the initial implementation of the network has about 1100 staff members, who have access to the communications network through a central message center.

EMS service began in 1983. About 120 telex messages per day are sent and received. About 250 pages of direct connect traffic are transmitted between the two primary sites per month. Future expansion plans include the addition of two more UL facilities to the direct connect network, one with 2500 staff and one with 1200.

Minimal problems were encountered in the start-up. Some communications protocol difficulties were experienced in setting up the modems and configuring the software settings appropriately for direct transmission and for connection to the ITT computer, but these were resolved through experimentation.

Centralization of the message function in each facility and limitation of initial implementation to just two locations minimized impact on staff and eased the break-in process. Using existing equipment and upgrading the mode of access to a familiar communications system also lessened training requirements and made for a smooth transition. There was little change in volume of message traffic during the early phases of implementation; volume increased gradually as the user community experienced improved message delivery speed.

Conclusions

Satisfaction with the system is high. The current configuration is appropriate to current needs and can be expanded to allow for growth of the communications network. By taking a gradual approach to the implementation, UL avoided the staff tension that is common with the introduction of new technology.

While the configuration chosen is relatively unsophisticated in that it does not provide the message handling capabilities of a CBMS or microcomputer-based system, it does meet the needs of this message environment. Since a centralized message switching function is provided by the word processing staff at each location and since the system is not designed for sending private messages individual access to the electronic mail system and private mailboxes for each user are not required. The UL configuration is an example of an appropriate match of system function and performance with real messaging needs.

UNITING FRAGMENTED COMMUNICATIONS THROUGH A CBMS

Background

Apple Computer, Inc. began to use EMS in 1981. At that time the company had 6000 employees, manufacturing facilities throughout the U.S. and was in the process of establishing plants abroad. As rapid growth was taking place within each division, various communications systems started springing up, resulting in the problem that none of these divisional systems could communicate with each other.

There were six types of communications systems in use at Apple at the time of EMS implementation. The voice (telephone) system had the most users. The internal mail (postal) department delivered thousands of letters daily. The data network had hundreds of online/dial-up users. The sales and marketing group had its own direct-dial connect EMS which used Apple IIs (programmed to call each other during non-business hours to take advantage of AT&T's lower rates) throughout the United States. The distribution group used the telex network. The corporate message center also used the telex/TWX network. There were also a few facsimile machines (domestic and international in place).

The decision was made to eliminate the fragmented communications approach with a CBMS, which could be accessed from the corporate data network.

The anticipated advantages included: 1.) improved communications between Apple locations worldwide; 2.) improved communications between Apple and its vendors/distributors; and 3.) utilization of Apple products internally. It was also expected that communications costs spent on a variety of transmission modes such as telephone, telex, telegram and mail could be reduced, while employee productivity was increased through the reduction of "telephone tag" (calling a party, missing them and vice versa).

System Chosen

After evaluating the available computer-based message systems, Apple determined that Tymshare's OnTyme II was best suited for its needs. No additional onsite equipment or software would be required, and the existing data network had already been linked to Tymnet.

The two basic pieces of hardware chosen for EMS implementation were the Apple II and Apple III microcomputers. Existing data terminals have been replaced with Apple IIIs using Access software. This allows the user to access both the data and EMS networks using the same equipment. The Apple III also allows users to have storage devices at their workstations. A user can upload data at a high speed, go off line and generate a report, then download the information into the EMS for delivery to another location within minutes (instead of days), and without the need to generate a stack of printouts.

Since Apple IIs can also work with OnTyme, many users who did not need to access the data network did not change to the Apple III until they needed larger storage capacity. The Micro/Courier and ASCII Express software packages are used on the Apple IIs. Most telex lines have been cancelled and the telex terminals have been replaced with Apple IIIs.

Implementation

The Corporate Telecommunications department (which was part of the MIS group) was chartered with the responsibility of planning, implementing and managing the new Apple EMS project. The initial implementation plan was to incorporate users of the existing fragmented systems. This included the marketing, distribution and MIS groups. Within nine months, a total of 750 users had been brought online. Planning included training classes, internal company newspaper articles and on-site training.

Conclusions

There are many reasons why EMS caught on so quickly. One important factor was that every department already had at least an Apple II, and many employees had a microcomputer at home. At the time, the company only used about 20 typewriters—most word processing was already being done using microcomputers. Selling the concept of electronically transmitting the document, instead of using the company mail system or the U.S. Postal Service, was not difficult. Of particular importance was the fact that upper management was involved in the approval process and initial use.

The largest problem during implementation was the very rapid acceptance of the system. The demand for the system to be brought up "immediately" caused a few time-management problems.

IMPLEMENTING AN EMS WITH INTELLIGENT PERIPHERALS

Background

The Bay Area Library Information Service (BALIS) is a cooperative agency comprising nine public libraries within a three-county area. The total number of employees is just over 1000, located in 10 central libraries and 25 branches. The communications budget in fiscal year 1983-1984 was approximately $17,000.

The BALIS system had been using TWX and courier services for several years to transmit messages and materials from one facility to another. Steadily rising TWX costs provided the incentive to investigate other methods. There was also a desire for greater flexibility than TWX could provide.

The communications needs of the BALIS system members are primarily local; i.e., within their own three-county area. However, there is a need to communicate to other libraries in the state (primarily the State Library in Sacramento) and outside the state. Most messages are requests for the loan of library materials not available in the local collection and replies to those requests. These requests number several thousand per year for each library or about 60,000 per year for the system.

System Chosen

In 1982 the decision was made to implement electronic mail. Teleprinter terminals and intelligent modems were purchased for each of the 10 central libraries, and DDD lines were installed. The equipment was selected because it could be used both for access to a CBMS (since Tymeshare's OnTyme service was gaining widespread acceptance in the library community throughout the U.S.) and for direct station-to-station DDD messaging. The peripheral chosen incorporates a Bell 103/212 modem with auto-originate and autoanswer, 48K RAM storage and text editing software, an internal clock/calendar and auto-dialing for unattended transmission of stored messages. It also provides a forms capability for automatic formatting of messages. In addition BALIS acquired access to the CBMS (OnTyme) for each location.

Implementation

Responsibility for implementation of the new system was given to the Interlibrary Loan (ILL) staff at each location, with assistance and training from the BALIS headquarters staff.

The total implementation and training period lasting about six months, during which there was a noticeable level of stress. The staff who were being trained had no previous experience with automated systems or word processing equipment. Consequently there was a noticeable drop in productivity levels (items processed per hour). Almost a year elapsed before productivity returned to its former level.

Most locations found that there was little resistance from local staff to the new system, but many complaints were made about the documentation provided by the hardware manufacturers. Simultaneous installation at all 10 locations meant that everyone was struggling to learn the system at the same time, and no one was able to benefit from the experience of others. Other problems occurred because personnel were attempting to learn the CBMS' commands at the same time that they were learning the procedures for station-to-station DDD messaging.

Effect on Communications Costs

The BALIS system attempted to record the number of items processed and the communications costs over a 16-month period, covering the transition from TWX-based operation to a combination DDD and CBMS operation. No records were available on the number of messages (as opposed to items) sent or received during the period under study.

Overall monthly communications costs dropped from a high of $2981 for TWX alone (in early 1982) to $1111 for the combined DDD/CBMS operation (in mid-1983). This dramatic reduction in costs, however, was accompanied by a similar drop in the number of items processed. The cost per item processed fell by only 20%. This still represents a substantial savings for BALIS and must be evaluated within the context of steadily rising costs for TWX and other leased-line services. The savings, when judged against what BALIS' costs would have become had they not invested in newer technology, are much greater.

Conclusions

Satisfaction with the hardware chosen is good. Although the documentation was criticized, support from the vendor was rated as excellent. Communications costs were significantly less than what they had been for the previous (TWX) system. Were the selection to be made again, BALIS would try to find hardware that allowed for much larger local memory capacity. The only other frequent criticism has been the sensitivity of the equipment to telephone line disturbances; so far, this problem has not been resolved.

Were the project to be repeated, however, several changes would be made. The most important would be in the schedule for implementation. Many of the problems that were encountered could have been avoided if the new equipment had been installed in one or two locations initially, with the remainder coming on over several months. This would have allowed the headquarters staff time to gain expertise and provide greater assistance and training to the other locations. Another change would be to delay access to the CBMS service until all the locations had several months of experience with the station-to-station DDD operations. The staff found it very difficult and confusing to learn both systems simultaneously.

Appendix B: Directory of Suppliers

COMMUNICATING WORD PROCESSOR SOFTWARE VENDORS

GRAPHNET TELEMARKETING
8230 Boone Blvd., Suite 330
Vienna, VA 22180
(800) 336-3729

NCR CORP.
335 Old Tarrytown Rd.
White Plains, NY 10603
(914) 428-2500

WANG LABORATORIES INC.
1 Industrial Ave.
Lowell, MA 01851
(617) 459-5000

INTELLIGENT PERIPHERAL DEVICES

BETACOM
245 E. Sixth St., Suite 814
St. Paul, MN 55101
(612) 292-8188

CYGNET TECHNOLOGIES, INC.
1296 Lawrence Station Rd.
Sunnyvale, CA 94089
(408) 734-9946

MICROCOM, INC.
1400 A Providence Highway
Norwood, MA 02062
(617) 762-9310

TELEFACE CORP.
111 Rivington St.
New York, NY 10002
(212) 477-6802

VISIONARY ELECTRONICS
141 Parker Ave.
San Francisco, CA 94118
(415) 751-8811

INTERCONNECTION SERVICE VENDORS

GENERAL VIDEOTEX CORP.
377 Putnam Ave.
Cambridge, MA 02125
(617) 491-3393

INTERNATIONAL ELECTRONIC MAIL SERVICE (IEMS)
21686 Stevens Creek Blvd.
Cupertino, CA 95014
(408) 446-4367

ITT BUSINESS COMMUNICATIONS
10 E. 40th St.
New York, NY 10017
(212) 532-4700

WESTERN UNION CORP.
1 Lake St.
Upper Saddle River, NY 07458
(800) 526-4680

MAJOR CBMS SERVICES

DIALCOM
ITT Dialcom, Inc.
1109 Spring St.
Silver Spring, MD 20910
(301) 588-1572

INFOPLEX
CompuServe, Inc.
5000 Arlington Centre Blvd.
PO Box 20212
Columbus, OH 43220
(614) 457-8600

MCI MAIL
2000 M. St. NW
Washington, DC 20036
(800) MCI-2255

ONTYME II
Tymshare, Inc.
20705 Valley Green Dr.
Cupertino, CA 95014
(408) 446-6000

SOURCEMAIL
Source Telecomputing Corp.
1616 Anderson Rd.
McLean, VA 22102
(703) 734-7500

TELEMAIL
GTE Telenet
8229 Boone Blvd.
Vienna, VA 22180
(703) 442-1000

MESSAGE PROCESSING WORKSTATIONS

AMERICAN TELEPROCESSING CORP.
10681 Haddington, Suite 100
Houston, TX 77043
(713) 868-5809

BASIC TELECOMMUNICATIONS CORP.
4414 E. Harmony Rd.
Fort Collins, CO 80525
(303) 226-4688

CARTERFONE COMMUNICATIONS CORP.
1111 W. Mockingbird Lane, Suite 1400
Dallas, TX 75247
(214) 630-9700

C&W INCOTEL, LTD.
One Penn Plaza
New York, NY 10119
(212) 594-8340

EXTEL CORP.
4000 Commercial Ave.
Northbrook, IL 60062
(312) 291-2500

HENRIKSEN DATA SYSTEMS, INC.
12325 W. 52nd Ave.
Wheat Ridge, CO 80033
(303) 425-9303

PERSONAL COMPUTER EMS SOFTWARE

MICROCOM, INC.
1400 A Providence Highway
Norwood, MA 02062
(617) 762-9310

SOFTWARE CONNECTIONS, INC.
2041 Mission College Blvd., Suite 135
Santa Clara, CA 95054
(408) 988-3704

TRANSEND CORP.
2190 Paragon Dr.
San Jose, CA 95131
(408) 946-7400

VECTOR GRAPHICS, INC.
500 N. Ventu Park Rd.
Thousand Oaks, CA 91320
(805) 499-5831

TWX/TELEX EMULATION SOFTWARE

ADVANCED MICRO TECHNIQUES
1291 E. Hillsdale Blvd., Suite 210
Foster City, CA 94404
(415) 349-9336

CAPPCOMM SOFTWARE, INC.
One World Trade Center, Suite 1453
New York, NY 10048
(212) 938-5702

CAWTHON SCIENTIFIC GROUP
24224 Michigan Ave.
Dearborn, MI 48124
(313) 565-4000

MICROCOM, INC.
1400 A Providence Highway
Norwood, MA 02062
(617) 762-9310

SGS SEMICONDUCTOR CORP.
1000 E. Bell Rd.
Phoenix, AZ 85022
(602) 867-6100

SOFTEST, INC.
555 Goffle Rd.
Ridgewood, NJ 07450
(201) 447-3901

Glossary*

Address: The coded representation of a destination terminal.

Analog: Signals that make use of varying voltages or tones to produce a continuous rather than a pulsed or digital signal. Traditionally, the telephone voice network has used analog signals. See also *Digital.*

Answerback: The response of a terminal to control signals from a sending station. An identifying code, unique to each station, transmitted (often automatically) upon receipt of a "Who are you?" signal.

ASCII: American Standard Code for Information Interchange. A code used to exchange data between computers. The "full ASCII" set has 96 alphanumeric and 32 control (nonprinting) characters.

Asynchronous: A transmission method that uses "start" and "stop" bits to indicate the beginning and end of each character. The characters do not have to be transmitted at regular time intervals, nor does the interval need to be a fixed length.

Autoanswer: An equipment feature that allows a station to automatically detect and respond to an incoming call.

Bandwidth: The range of frequencies available for transmitting. Usually expressed as the difference (in cycles per second, or Hertz) between the highest and lowest frequencies of the band.

Baseband: A single-channel medium, using non-modulated frequencies. Generally used for digitized signals over short distances.

Baud: A unit of signaling speed equivalent to the number of signaling events per second. Sometimes used (incorrectly) interchangeably with BPS.

Baudot: A code for data transmission which uses five bits to represent each character. Used on the telex network.

---

*This glossary uses terms and definitions from the "Telecommunications Glossary," prepared by the Cooperative Library Agency for Systems and Services (CLASS).

Binary: A system which permits the selection of two distinct and exclusive possibilities, for example "0" and "1" or positive and negative impulses.

Bit rate: The rate at which bits (binary digits) are transmitted. See *BPS*.

Blocking: When no paths or circuits are available to complete a call and a busy tone is received by the calling party. Sometimes termed a "busy out" condition.

BPS: Bits Per Second. The rate at which bits are transmitted. Applied both to the transmission channel and to the devices attached to it. Also expressed in Kilobits per second (KBPS) and Megabits per second (MBPS).

Broadband: A communications path with large bandwidth, and therefore capable of greater data-carrying capacity. Often a multiple-channel medium, as with cable television systems, and able to carry simultaneous video, voice and data signals on different channels.

Broadcast: The simultaneous transmission to all stations on a system.

Buffer: A temporary storage area or memory used to compensate for differences in the rate of data flow when transmitting from one device to another.

Byte: A unit of measurement of information, roughly one character (letter, number, space). Used for describing memory capacity, usually expressed as "K" or "kilobytes" (1024 bytes); also as "M" or "megabytes" (1,048,976 bytes).

CBMS: Computer Based Message System. A type of electronic mailbox service which uses a central computer to store and manipulate messages.

CCITT: Consultative Committee for International Telegraph and Telephone. An advisory group which recommends international standards.

Channel: A means of communication between two or more points. Also called a circuit, line, link, path, facility.

Common carrier: Any company which furnishes communications services to the general public, and which is regulated by appropriate federal state or local agencies.

Conditioning: The addition of equipment to a leased voice-grade channel in order to provide the appropriate line characteristics required for data transmission.

Contention: A method of line control in which terminals request permission to transmit. If the channel is free, transmission goes ahead; otherwise, the terminal must wait until it becomes free. This method is used by some LANs (local area networks).

Control character: A nonprinting code or character which, when transmitted, is an instruction to start, modify or stop a control function. Examples include: carriage return, form feed, send answerback, disconnect line.

DDD: Direct Distance Dialing. The making of toll calls on the public telephone network without an operator's assistance. Also refers to the network itself.

Dedicated line: A telephone line reserved for the exclusive use of one customer. Also called a *Leased line.*

Dial-up: A system using manual or automatic dialing to establish the routing of a call through a public switched network. The circuit is maintained only for the duration of the transmission.

Digital: A discrete, discontinuous, on-or-off signal. Telephone systems are now converting from analog to digital.

Duplex: The capability of transmitting in two directions on the same communications *channel*, either simultaneously (full-duplex) or alternately (half-duplex).

EBCDIC: Extended Binary Coded Decimal Interchange Code. A code using eight bits per character, commonly used on IBM systems.

EIA RS-232: The standard interface established by the Electronics Industry Association (EIA) for the connection between a modem and a communications line.

FAX: Facsimile Exchange. The transmission of pictures or documents over communications channels. The image is scanned at the transmitting site and converted into computer-readable signals. It is reconstructed at the receiving station, to be duplicated on paper.

FEX: Foreign Exchange. Service that connects a customer's telephone to a telephone company's central office other than the one normally servicing the customer's location. FEX provides out-of-town callers with a local (i.e., toll free) number.

Gateway: Any service which provides an interconnection between two dissimilar networks or services, or between those which do not normally connect because of their proprietary status.

Handshake: The line interplay which is used to establish a data-communications path; the exchange of predetermined signals by the calling and receiving modems.

Hertz: Measure of frequency or bandwidth; same as cycles per second.

IRC: International Record Carrier. Any company which provides worldwide telecommunications transmission services, excluding oral communications.

LAN: Local Area Network. A communications system that connects computers, terminals or workstations within a limited geographic area. The transmission medium may be twisted pair wire, optical fiber or coaxial cable.

Leased line: A communications circuit designated to be for the exclusive use of a subscriber. Also called private line.

Local loop: The telephone lines connecting the customer's premises to the telephone company's central office.

Microprocessor: A single computer chip central processing unit (CPU).

Modem: Contraction of modulator/demodulator. A device which converts digital pulses from a computer or terminal to frequencies which can be transmitted on analog communications lines. The reverse process must be done at the receiving end, so modems always operate in pairs. On a digital communications path, no conversion is necessary so modems are not required.

Multi-address: The routing of a message to more than one destination or station in a network.

Multiplex: The division of a communications line into two or more channels. This can be done either by splitting the frequency band into narrower bands or by allocating the single frequency to each user in turn. Multiplexing greatly increases the efficiency of the communications line by allowing it to carry more data.

Network architecture: Used to describe the way points in a network are connected to each other. Three popular configurations are a star (where all messages pass through a central hub), a ring (where messages are passed around a continuous loop to their destination), and a bus or chain (where each station is in line).

Nonprinting character: A control character, transmitted as part of the data, but not generally displayable by the receiving equipment.

Packet switching: A technique whereby long messages are subdivided into short packets with a fixed maximum length. This contrasts with conventional switching methods where messages are transmitted whole, irrespective of length. Tymnet, Telenet and Uninet all use packet switching methods.

Online: Refers to any equipment under the direct control of the CPU. Also, the ability of a user to access the computer and interact with it through a terminal.

Parallel: A form of data transmission in which all of the bits making up a character are sent concurrently rather than sequentially. It requires the use of multiple channels or multiple frequencies on the same channel. Contrast with *Serial.*

PBX: Private Branch Exchange. A telephone exchange installed on a customer's premises and operated by the customer. It allows both internal dialing from station to station within the customer's premises and connection to the public telephone network. A PBX may be manual, automatic (PABX) or computerized (CBX).

Point-to-point: A transmission or network which connects the sending and receiving stations directly, not through an intermediate station or device.

Polling: Any procedure that sequentially contacts each point or terminal on a communications line to see if that terminal has data to send. Polling is an alternative to contention, and insures that no terminal is kept waiting too long.

Protocol: Any formal set of conventions governing the format and control of data exchanged between two devices.

Public switched network: Any common carrier network that provides circuit switching between all users. Includes the TWX, telex and telephone networks.

Real time: Data processing which occurs at a rate sufficient to allow responses to be immediately usable in the processing.

Response time: The time lapse between a message transmission and the arrival of a reply. Usually applies to interactive computer systems.

RS-232: See *EIA RS-232.*

Serial: A form of data transmission in which nonsimultaneous signals are sent sequentially at intervals, with or without synchronization.

Store-and-forward: Applied to communication systems in which messages are received at intermediate points and stored. They are then retransmitted to a further point or to the ultimate destination. No direct connection between sender and recipient is established.

Switch: Any device which controls and assigns the communications paths within a network.

Switched network: A network in which the individual stations are not permanently linked. Connections are established as needed, then disconnected. The telephone system is an example of a switched network, as are TWX and telex.

Synchronous: A form of transmission in which data are sent continuously using a timing rate shared by both terminals.

Telex: The international public switched teletype network.

Terminal: Any device capable of sending or receiving over a communications channel.

Text editor: A line-oriented program which allows the data or text within a message to be modified a single line at a time. This is in contrast to a word processor, which generally allows the cursor to be moved about the full screen very rapidly, and which can modify several lines of text simultaneously.

TWX: Typewriter Exchange Service. The North American teleprinter exchange service run by Western Union. It is a switched network, and provides direct connections between subscribers. TWX service is also called Telex II.

Unattended operation: Any feature which allows the transmission and/or receipt of messages without assistance from a person.

Van: Valued Added Network. A common carrier, such as Tymnet or Telenet, which adds additional services (protocol conversion, speed conversion, etc.) to its data transmission services.

Voice-grade channel: A channel suitable for the transmission of speech, digital or analog data, or facsimile, generally having a frequency range of about 300 to 3000 Hertz.

Wideband: The term applied to channels provided by common carriers capable of transferring data at speeds from 19,200 bps up to 1 million bps.

Bibliography

"A Year of Living Uncertainly: Outlook '84 Office Automation Systems." *Modern Office Technology* 29 (1) (January 1984): 42-44.

Berger, Myron. "Message for Owners of PCs: Modem links you to Telex." *Wall Street Computer Review* (September/October 1983): 69.

Bolger, William. "USPS and Mailers Can Be Partners in Progress." *ZIP* 6 (1) (January 1983): 25, 35-36.

"Computer Mail Effort Abandoned." *New York Times* (June 6, 1984).

Connell, Stephen, and Galbraith, Ian A. *Electronic Mail: A Revolution in Business Communications*. White Plains, NY: Knowledge Industry Publications, Inc., 1982.

Electronic Mail. Framingham, MA: International Data Corp., 1983.

FitzGerald, Jerry, and Eason, Tom S. *Fundamentals of Data Communications.* New York: John Wiley & Sons, 1978.

Frank, Ronald A. "Computerized Mail Seen Future Benefit." *Computerworld* 12 (41) (October 1978): 18, 23.

Hafner, K. "Study Examines Future of OA Market." *Computerworld* 17 (36) (September 5, 1983): 73.

Hayword, M. "The WP Solution." *Computerworld* 17 (16A) (April 20, 1983): 49-51.

Levinger, Jeffrey Emmet, and Merges, Robert Patrick. *Visiterm User's Guide*. San Jose, CA: VisiCorp Inc., 1982.

Mathison, Stuart L. "Telecommunications: Linking up for Greater Productivity." *Administrative Management* 42 (3) (March 1981): 33-34, 74.

Mercer, Ronald. "Office Automation: Managers Will Have to Change." *Computing Canada* 9 (8) (April 1983): 15, 24-25.

Reaume, Lloyd. "Terminals, Telephones and Technology." *Computer Data* 8 (4) (April 1983): 4-5.

Index

About the Authors

Libby Trudell is marketing manager for Dialog Information Services, Inc. Previously, she was the senior coordinator for the Cooperative Library Agency for Systems and Services (CLASS) and research analyst for the New England Library Information Network (NELINET). Ms. Trudell's articles have appeared in a number of professional journals, including *Online* and *Library Hi Tech.* She is a member of the American Library Association and is on the editorial board of *Library Hi Tech.* Ms. Trudell is a graduate of Tufts University and holds an M.S. in Library Science from Simmons College.

Janet Bruman is product manager, Cooperative Library Agency for Systems and Services (CLASS), San Jose, CA. **Dennis Oliver** is president of International Electronic Mail Service (IEMS), Cupertino, CA, which provides a variety of communication and interconnection services.